The ENGAGED SOCIOLOGIST

*This book is dedicated to the memory of
Aiden Tomkins Odell and to all the families
working to find a cure for spinal muscular atrophy (SMA).*

*You can learn about SMA and how to help find a
cure by going to http://www.fsma.org/*

*To read Aiden's story, go to http://www.fsma.org/
photoalbum/memorial/odell.shtml*

The ENGAGED SOCIOLOGIST

Connecting the Classroom to the Community

Kathleen Korgen
William Paterson University

Jonathan M. White
Bridgewater State College

PINE FORGE PRESS
An Imprint of Sage Publications, Inc.
Thousand Oaks • London • New Delhi

For information:

Pine Forge Press
An Imprint of Sage Publications, Inc.
2455 Teller Road
Thousand Oaks, California 91320
E-mail: order@sagepub.com

Sage Publications Ltd.
1 Oliver's Yard
55 City Road
London EC1Y 1SP
United Kingdom

Sage Publications India Pvt. Ltd.
B-42, Panchsheel Enclave
Post Box 4109
New Delhi 110 017 India

Printed in the United States of America

Library of Congress Cataloging-in-Publication Data

Korgen, Kathleen Odell, 1967-
The engaged sociologist: connecting the classroom to the community/
Kathleen Korgen, Jonathan M. White.
     p. cm.
Includes bibliographical references and index.
ISBN 1-4129-3659-4 or 978-1-4129-3659-0 (pbk).

    1. Student service—United States. 2. Sociology—Study and teaching
(Higher)—United States. I. White, Jonathan. II. Title.
LC221.K68 2007
301.071'173—dc22

                                                    2006015093

This book is printed on acid-free paper.

06   07   08   09   10   10   9   8   7   6   5   4   3   2   1

Acquisitions Editor:	Ben Penner
Editorial Assistant:	Camille Herrera
Production Editor:	Catherine M. Chilton
Copy Editor:	Edward Meidenbauer
Typesetter:	C&M Digitals (P) Ltd.
Proofreader:	Jennifer Ang
Indexer:	Kirsten Kite
Cover Designer:	Candice Harman

Contents

Preface

A Note From the Authors to the Students Reading This Book

Sociology is the coolest academic discipline. Seriously, what other area of study is better at helping you figure out how society operates and how you can use that knowledge to create social change? Both of us were drawn to sociology because we wanted to figure out how to fight injustice and promote democracy more effectively. It has also guided us with everyday life tasks, such as figuring out how to get policies passed on campus, deciding who to vote for, and learning why it's vital to earn a college degree in a service-based economy. This book is part of our efforts to get students hooked on sociology and, in the process, help them to become engaged and effective citizens who can strengthen our democratic society.

This book is also part of a larger, national effort to "educate citizens" by encouraging students to participate in civic engagement exercises that connect the classroom to the community. Organizations like Campus Compact and the American Democracy Project are establishing movements to make civic engagement a part of the college experience for all undergraduates. College leaders all across the country realize that we are obligated to give students the tools they will require to be effective citizens as well as the skills they will need in the workforce. Leaders in *all* sectors of society understand that higher education, when connected to the larger society, benefits everyone on *and* off campus.

We believe, as leaders of The American Sociological Association have noted when promoting public sociology, that sociology is particularly suited to teaching students what they need to become effective and full members of our society. As prominent sociologist Randall Collins has pointed out, the two core commitments of sociology are (a) to understand how sociology works and (b) to use that knowledge to make society better. We believe that helping students learn how to think sociologically and use sociological tools is, in effect, enabling them to become better citizens. No doubt, the professors who assigned this book to you also share this belief. They will gladly tell you why *they* think sociology is an incredibly useful and practical academic discipline.

We also know that sociology is fun to learn and to teach. That's why we created a book that's enjoyable to use for both students and teachers. The exercises throughout the chapters allow students to connect the sociological knowledge they are learning to their campus and the larger community. So, as soon as you develop your sociological eye you will make use of it! *Please note that you will need to make sure you follow the rules for research on human subjects and get approval from the Internal Review Board on your campus (IRB) before carrying out some of these exercises* (your professor will tell you how to do so). This book will also help you to connect your own life to the larger society, as you learn about the "sociological imagination" and the power it has to positively affect your community. The Sociologist in Action sections in each chapter will show you powerful examples of how sociology students and professional sociologists (both professors and applied sociologists) use sociology in myriad ways in efforts to improve society. By the end of the book, you can create your own Sociologist in Action section, in which you'll show how you used sociological tools in efforts to influence society.

We look forward to seeing your Sociology in Action pieces and featuring many of them in future editions of this book and on the *The Engaged Sociologist's* Web site. In the meantime, we hope you enjoy the book and use the knowledge and skills you gain from it to make yourself a more effective citizen, strengthen our democracy, and work for a more just and civil society. We think that you will discover what we discovered when we began our journey as sociologists—that sociology is a cool and powerful tool. And, of course, we hope that you have a lot of fun in the process!

Acknowledgments

Wᵉ would like to thank Ben Penner, our editor, for his excellent work and for believing in the vision of this book. His enthusiasm for *The Engaged Sociologist* and public sociology, in general, inspired us as we conceptualized and wrote this book. We remain indebted to him for his good humor and his passion and insight regarding the powerful connections between sociology and student engagement. We also are indebted to Camille Herrera and Annie Louden, our Editorial Assistants, for their strong support and ability to guide us throughout the course of this project. We owe a special debt of gratitude to our colleague, Howard Lune, for his contributions to this book.

Finally, we would both like to thank the following reviewers whose thoughtful and excellent suggestions helped us make this book so much better than it otherwise would be:

Beverly L. Stiles, Midwestern State University

Stephen Light, SUNY Plattsburgh

Ronda Copher, University of Minnesota

Kooros M. Mahmoudi, Northern Arizona University

Amy Holzgang, Cerritos College

Peter J. Stein, William Paterson University

Eric K. Leung, Los Angeles Valley College

John Lynxwiler, The University of Central Florida

Kathleen would like to thank her encouraging and accommodating husband Jeff, daughters Julie and Jessica, and mother Patricia Odell, for putting up with the many late nights, early mornings, and weekends this project consumed. Jeff and Patricia also read innumerable early drafts with good cheer and made many helpful suggestions. This book would never have been completed on time if we didn't live together, Mom. Thank you!

Thanks also to Judy and Ben Korgen, Ann Odell, Mike Odell, John Odell, Nancy Baffa, and Conor Odell.

Jonathan would like to thank his beautiful wife Shelley for her incredible friendship, love, and support. It is because of you and our amazing partnership that I am able to continue moving forward as a public sociologist and with our many civic engagement projects. I know how lucky I am in this world to have found you. A huge thanks also goes to my family, who provide me with unwavering support, love, and happiness and who inspire me to continuously work toward creating a stronger civil society. And a very special group of people, my 11 nephews and nieces, deserve a special debt of gratitude because they are particularly inspirational in so many ways!

1

The Engaged Sociologist

*The Sociological Perspective
and the Connections Between
Sociology, Democracy, and Civic Engagement*

Have you ever wanted to change society? Do you want to have a voice in how things work throughout your life? If so, you've come to the right discipline. Sociology can help you to understand how society operates and, in turn, how to make it better.

As sociologists, we see how individuals both shape and are shaped by larger social forces. By developing what is called a sociological eye,[1] we are able to look beneath the surface of society and see how it really works. For example, with a sociological eye, we can recognize the tremendous influence of culture on individuals. Imagine how different you might be if you grew up in Sweden, Ethiopia, or Bangladesh.[2] You would still look about the same (though with different mannerisms, speaking a different language, and with a different haircut and clothes), but your values, norms, and beliefs would be different. Your view of the proper roles of men and women, your religious or secular values, career goals, education, and so forth would be shaped by the society in which you grew up.

Look at the differences between your immediate family and some of your relatives who have much more or much less money. Does social class cause the differences, or do the differences help to determine the social class to which we will belong?[3] Consider the different perspectives that your male relatives and your female relatives bring to the same questions. They all live in the same world, in close proximity even, but they have had such different experiences of it that some people see men and women as coming from different planets.[4]

By using the sociological eye, sociologists look at the world from a unique angle, notice what is often unobserved, and make connections among the patterns in everyday events that the average person might not notice. In doing so, we can understand how different organizations, institutions, and societies function, how social forces shape individual lives and ideas, and, in turn, how individuals shape organizations and institutions. This perspective enables us to notice when persistent patterns work to create disadvantages for certain groups in society, resulting in institutional discrimination (intentional or unintentional structural biases).

For example, our society functioned in such a way that there were no female Supreme Court Justices before President Ronald Reagan appointed Sandra Day O'Connor in 1981. Sociologists, using a sociological eye, recognize that the longstanding all-male makeup of the Supreme Court was part of a larger pattern of sex discrimination. Some of the discrimination was deliberate and based on people's ideas about gender. Some of it was political, based on a calculation of how the public would respond to the nomination of a woman to such a post. Some of it even had to do with the fact that our culture tends to use similar language and ideas to describe both "leadership qualities" and "masculinity." Thus, when people think of "leadership" they tend to associate it with the qualities that men often bring to the table.[5,6] Social science research on the connections between gender roles, socialization, and sex discrimination, such as Betty Friedan's book *The Feminine Mystique* (1963), which shattered the myth that women could only find fulfillment as wives and homemakers, became part of public knowledge and were used to make the case for the women's movement in the 1960s and 1970s. Ultimately, this movement paved the way for a political environment conducive to the appointment of Sandra Day O'Connor in 1981.

Use of the sociological eye also helps efforts to persuade government office holders to initiate social policies addressing social inequities. By looking beneath the surface of government operations we can answer the following questions: To whom do office holders tend to respond the most? Why? How can we use this information to make sure that they respond to us? What social forces compelled Ronald Reagan, one of our most conservative Presidents and not known as a women's rights advocate, to choose a female Supreme Court Justice?

According to Randall Collins, using the sociological eye is one of two "core commitments" of sociology.[7] The second is social activism. Once we understand how society operates, we are obligated to participate actively in efforts to improve it. The sociological eye and social activism go hand in hand. The sociological eye helps us to become effective, engaged citizens. The sociological eye is something we gain with training—much as muscles are gained with weight lifting and working out. The more you train yourself as a sociologist, the stronger your sociological eye and ability to practice effective and constructive social activism will become.

❖ THE SOCIOLOGICAL IMAGINATION

To understand how we might influence society, we must first realize how we are affected by it. C. Wright Mills described this ability as the "sociological imagination."[8] When we can relate personal troubles to public issues, connecting our individual lives to what's happening in our society, we are using the sociological imagination.

For instance, both of the authors of this book experienced their parents divorcing. As individuals, this was a personal trouble for each of us. Using the sociological imagination, we see that we were a part of a cohort of American children who lived through the great rise in the divorce rate in the 1970s. If we had been children during the 1870s, our parents would most likely have remained married. However, the changes that our society went through in the 1960s and 1970s (legal rights and protections for women that enabled more women to exit relationships, the decline of religiosity, cost of living increases that required more women to join the workforce, etc.) resulted in an increase in the divorce rate and, in turn, our own parents' divorces. Our personal troubles (the divorces of our parents) were directly related to a public issue (the society-wide rise in the divorce rate).

Today, one of us is having a difficult time finding clothes for her young daughters that do not resemble those in Paris Hilton's closet. As a mother, she's horrified that anyone would expect little girls to wear such skimpy outfits (particularly *her* little girls!). As a sociologist, she can look at a sample of clothing stores and advertisements in the United States and quickly realize that her experience is part of a society-wide pattern of sexualizing girls.[9] She can then start to research why a society like ours, with such a long history of public activism around "standards of moral decency" is so consistent—almost aggressive—in the sexualizing of girls. One hypothesis she might test is that this social behavior is related to the relative absence of women in the highest positions of government and the judiciary. If she were to find this to be true, she could use her findings to work for social change, trying to influence policy or to help build a movement that leads to more women in these important positions.

One of the functions of sociology, as C. Wright Mills defined it, "should be the transformation of private troubles into public issues."[10] Once you start using your sociological imagination and looking at the world through the sociological eye, it's impossible not to notice the connections between ourselves as individuals and patterns in society. Consider the kind of job you hope to get after leaving college. Will you make an annual salary or an hourly wage? Will you have full health care coverage, or will you live without insurance and hope for the best? And if you get the "good" job, will your good fortune depend some-how on the fact that others do not have what you seek? Are the private troubles of sweatshop workers also a public problem?

Sweatshops are mostly unregulated production sites where work-ers face near-slavery conditions with few or no protections from unsafe conditions or arbitrary punishments and at pay rates that are less than what one needs for basic survival. Sweatshop jobs do not come with insurance, pensions, or retirement plans—the built-in protections against the misfortunes that can befall any of us at any time. On the surface, colleges and sweatshops seem to have nothing to do with one another. However, if you look underneath the surface (or, perhaps, at what you or your classmates are wearing) you may see a connection! The students at Duke University saw a connection: When they learned of the horrible sweatshop conditions in which most of their clothes were being manufactured, they mobilized and established a Students Against Sweatshops group on campus. Their efforts, and those of sev-eral administrators at Duke (particularly the Director of Duke Store Operations), sparked a campus-wide discussion about sweatshops and the university's responsibility to ensure that clothing with a Duke label is "sweat free."

In 1997, Duke was the first institution of higher education in the United States to adopt a code of conduct mandating that the apparel companies with which they do business must submit to independent monitoring of the conditions in their factories. The following year, Duke established an independent Worker Rights Consortium (WRC) to assist in the enforcement of the codes of conduct established between colleges and universities and those who manufacture clothes for them.[11] As of 2005, 148 institutions of higher education had joined the movement sparked by Duke students and become WRC affiliates.[12]

❖ SOCIOLOGY AND THE CRITICAL CONSUMPTION OF INFORMATION

In addition to having a sociological eye and making use of the sociological imagination, sociologists are informed and critical consumers of the barrage of information coming at us from all directions. Sociological research methods guide how we conduct research and how we interpret information relayed by others. By understanding how good research is done, we can evaluate the information disseminated throughout society and know what news sources are trustworthy. These skills help us in our efforts to both understand and change society. In Chapter 3, we outline in greater detail how sociological research methods can be used in this way.

❖ SOCIOLOGY AND DEMOCRACY

Through reading this book and carrying out the exercises within it, you will learn how to look beneath the surface of social events, connect personal troubles to public issues, and know what information sources are trustworthy. You can then use these sociological tools to strengthen our society, make our nation more democratic, and work toward ensuring the rights and well-being of people all around the world. Democracy is defined in different ways by a multitude of scholars. However, all point out that it is a system of governance that instills state power in citizenship rather than in government. This book shows how sociology can enable citizens to become knowledgeable, active, and effective participants in our democratic society.

Exercise 1.1	Walking Billboards

You occupy many "social roles" in your life: You are a student, somebody's friend, somebody's child, and maybe you are a parent, sibling, employee, teammate, boss, neighbor, or mentor. To many thousands of companies out there, your main role is that of "consumer." How do apparel companies market themselves, specifically, to men, women, and different racial/ethnic groups? How do members of each of these groups act as "Walking Billboards" for the apparel companies that make the clothing they wear?

(Continued)

— (Continued)

Next time you are in one of your *other* classes, note the following:

1. How many students are there? How many male, how many female?

2. How many of each is wearing visible product or company logos on their clothing? (Include yourself in your answers.)

3. Are there any logos that occur more than once throughout the class?

4. Are there any logos or brands that are considered "in" on your campus?

5. Using your newly trained "sociological eye," analyze the results you have gathered. What institutional and societal forces might be at work? Do you notice any specific trends along race or gender lines? Do certain people from different sex or racial/ethnic groups, teams, or cliques exhibit trends in their dress? How about the faculty? Do you detect any trends among your teachers?

Exercise 1.2	What's the Connection Between College Students and Sweatshops?

1. Watch the online video "Sweating for a T-Shirt" from United Students Against Sweatshops at http://www.freespeech.org/fscm2/ramgen.php? url=rtsp%3A%2F%2Frealmedia.freespeech.org%2FSweating_4_ T-shirt.rm%2FSweating_4_T-shirt.rm

2. Find out if your campus belongs to the Fair Labor Association (FLA). You can find this out at http://www.fairlabor.org/all/colleges/list.html

3. If not, find out what vendors your campus bookstore uses to obtain the clothes they sell.

4. Ask the campus bookstore manager if he or she is aware of the working conditions under which the vendors' employees work.

5. Do some research to find information about the vendors. The United Students Against Sweatshop's Sweat Free Campus campaign website that you can access through http://www.studentsagainstsweatshops.org/ campaigns.php is one useful site. Then, check out the website for Business and Human Rights Resource Center and Responsible Shopper (Coop America) at http://www.business-humanrights.org/Categories/Individual companies and http://www.responsibleshopper.org

6. Write a report on the results of your research that makes the link between campus consumerism and the workers who make the apparel sold in the campus bookstore.

7. Extra Credit: Find out where your school's teams get their jerseys, and repeat the exercises above.

Exercise 1.3   How Is Higher Education Related to Democracy?

If you live in a democracy, then you have inherited certain social obligations. What do you think they are? Is voting one of them? How about going to college? Is going to college a "social obligation"?

1. What do you think is the purpose of higher education?

2. Why did you decide to go to college?

3. Do you think your college education will help you become a better citizen? Why or why not?

4. Now go to the American Association of State Colleges and Universities (AASCU)'s Web site at http://aascu.org/.

5. Did your answer to question #1 relate to the AASCU's description of the purpose of public higher education? Why do you think it did or did not?

6. Why is an educated public necessary for a strong democratic society?

7. Is a public higher education attainable for all Americans? Why or why not? If not, what are the ramifications of this situation for our democracy? How can you, using what your sociological eye has uncovered, work to make public higher education more attainable and realizable for more people?

Exercise 1.4   Worried About the Increasingly High Cost of Tuition?

You are not alone. According to the College Board, "over the ten-year period ending in 2002–2003, *after adjusting for inflation,* average tuition and fees at both public and private four-year colleges and universities rose 38 percent."[13] Since 2003, tuitions at both private and public universities increased even further.

(Continued)

(Continued)

1. How would strategies to deal with the increase in tuition vary depending on whether it is viewed as (a) a personal trouble or (b) a public issue?

2. What are some of the actions you could take to convince state legislators to increase funding for public higher education in your state?

3. Choose one of the actions you've listed in question 2 that is a manageable action for you to take. Now, carry out the plan you devised and write a report that describes (a) what you did and (b) the outcome of your actions. Note that you might have to wait a while to complete (b), so you should start (a) right away.

Sociologist in Action: Diane Vaughan

Diane Vaughan, a professor of sociology at Boston College, has used the sociological eye to see patterns in such varied places as marital breakups and NASA disasters. Her widely acclaimed book, *The Challenger Launch Decision: Risky Technology, Culture, and Deviance at NASA* (1996), led to widespread media attention and to her highly publicized work as a consultant for the Commission assigned to investigate what led to the catastrophic reentry of the *Columbia* on February 1, 2003. In the following paragraph, she vividly describes how she viewed the *Columbia* accident through a sociological lens.

A few days after the accident, I was riveted by NASA's televised revelation about the *Columbia* foam strike and the long history of foam debris from the External Tank hitting the Orbiter. O-ring erosion responsible for *Challenger* also had a long problem history prior to that accident. Next day, the Space Shuttle Program Manager, face etched with grief and fatigue, showed a large piece of foam the size of the one that struck *Columbia*. Discounting its importance as a probable cause, he acknowledged repeated foam debris hits to the wings by explaining, ". . . we were comfortable with it." I was astonished. The normalization of deviance—a key concept from my *Challenger* research explaining how NASA first accepted an O-ring anomaly, then accepted more and more, until flying with damaged O-rings became normal and routine—seemed to fit this second accident scenario. NASA's former Solid Rocket Booster Manager, who played a major role in the *Challenger* launch decision and with whom I had lost contact, fired me an e-mail with subject head, "Déjà Vu All Over Again!" Media inquiries ballooned. Defining this as a professional responsibility and teaching opportunity, I tried to respond to every inquiry. What I was teaching was the sociological perspective, using the theory and concepts that explained *Challenger*. In the first few weeks, many reporters were new to the space beat, so knew nothing about the first accident or how NASA worked. Others, because they usually covered NASA, had read my book, and/or had interviewed me when the book was published, knew all too well. Like me, they quickly saw parallels between *Challenger* and *Columbia*.[14]

Vaughan, and the reporters who had read her work, noticed the parallels because they were looking at the two disasters with the sociological eye. In doing so, they were able to see the similarities between the underlying patterns of the two tragedies. Whereas most onlookers could just see that mistakes were made by NASA employees that resulted in two separate tragedies, those who looked at the disasters from a sociological perspective could trace the patterns of both mistakes and see the consistencies. Fulfilling the second core commitment of sociology, social activism, Vaughan publicized her findings and provided useful information for NASA personnel as they attempt to avoid future catastrophes of this nature.

❖ DISCUSSION QUESTIONS

1. Before reading this chapter, had you ever recognized a connection between your own life and the lives of people working in sweatshops? Why or why not? Do you see one now? Now that you have thought about this, how will you proceed?

2. Are you worried about being able to obtain adequate health care coverage? Why or why not? What are some steps that you can take to work toward ensuring that you and others will have a better chance at adequate health care coverage in your lives? If you're unsure, look at the plan proposed by the American Academy of Family Physicians at http://www.aafp.org/x13722.xml. Will you work toward this end and, if so, how?

3. Do you know what your President, Senators, and Representatives are doing about (a) sweatshops and (b) adequate health care? If you don't know, why do you think you are unaware of their positions on these issues? Would (or have) their positions on these issues influenced whether or not you would vote for them? Why or why not?

4. Do you ever think you could do what Dianne Vaughan, the sociologist in action, has done? What makes you think so?

❖ SUGGESTIONS FOR SPECIFIC ACTIONS

1. Join an already established campus group working against sweatshops. (You may substitute a different issue or campaign if you are already involved or interested in one, with permission of your instructor.)

2. Establish your own campus group to fight sweatshops. Go to http://www.freethechildren.com/youthzone/makeithappen/startupkit.htm and http://www.studentsagainstsweatshops.org/getinvolved/join_committee.php to learn how to form a local group to combat sweatshops.

3. Go to your Representatives' and Senators' Web sites (you can find them at www.house.gov and http://www.senate.gov/). Send them an e-mail that conveys your thoughts and feelings about the health care coverage crisis.

4. Investigate the kind of health care coverage and the safety of the work–living environment provided for students, faculty, professional, and support staff on your campus. If there are clear deficiencies or inequities, organize a group of students, faculty, professional, and support staff to advocate for improved conditions for all campus workers. For the past few years, sociology students at the University of California at Berkeley have carried out just this type of research and activism. You can find "Berkeley's Betrayal: Wages and Working Conditions at CAL" at www.berkeleysbetrayal.org/.

Please go to our Web site at http://www.sagepub.com/korgen to find further civic engagement opportunities, resources, and peer-reviewed articles related to this chapter.

❖ ENDNOTES

1. Collins 1998.
2. If you did grow up in Sweden, Ethiopia, or Bangladesh, then imagine you grew up in New Jersey.
3. It works both ways, of course. And bonus points to you for looking at the endnote.
4. Gray 1992.
5. Schein 2001.

6. We should note that this view is less prevalent today than it was at the time of Sandra Day O'Connor's appointment to the Supreme Court.

7. Collins 1998.

8. Mills 1967.

9. Even very young girls.

10. Mills 1967.

11. To learn more about the history of the sweat-free campus movement at Duke, go to Paul Baerman's article at http://www.dukemagazine.duke.edu/alumni/dm18/sweatshop.html.

12. See the Worker Rights Consortium website at http://www.workersrights.org/as.asp.

13. See the House Education and the Workforce Committee Fact Sheet at http://edworkforce.house.gov/issues/108th/education/highereducation/factsheetcost101003.htm accessed on July 19, 2005.

14. Vaughan (under review).

❖ REFERENCES

Baerman, Paul. 1998. "Giving Voice to the Campus Conscience: Students Against Sweatshops." *Duke University Alumni Magazine.* Accessed at http://www.dukemagazine.duke.edu/alumni/dm18/sweatshop.html on January 11, 2006.

Collins, Randall. 1998. "The Sociological Eye and Its Blinders." *Contemporary Sociology* 27(1): 2–7.

Friedan, Betty. 1963. *The Feminine Mystique.* New York: W.W. Norton and Company.

Gray, John. 1992. *Men Are From Mars, Women Are From Venus: A Practical Guide for Improving Communication and Getting What You Want in Your Relationships.* New York: HarperCollins Publishers.

The House Education & Workforce Committee Fact Sheet. Accessed at http://edworkforce.house.gov/issues/108th/education/highereducation/factsheetcost101003.htm on July 19, 2005.

Mills, C. Wright. 1967. *The Sociological Imagination.* New York: Oxford University Press.

Schein, Virginia E. 2001. "A Global Look at Psychological Barriers to Women's Progress in Management." *Journal of Social Issues,* 57, 675–88.

Vaughan, Dianne. Under review. "NASA Revisited: Ethnography, Theory, and Public Sociology."

2

Founders and Foundations of Sociology

Theory

S ociology was founded by social scientists eager to (a) understand the major social changes of the late 19th and early 20th centuries and (b) make society better. In this chapter, you will learn about how five of the founders of Sociology—Karl Marx, Max Weber, Emile Durkheim, George Herbert Mead, and Jane Addams—carried out the two core commitments of sociology. Each of the theorists, in his or her own way, looked underneath the surface of society to understand how it operates and used this knowledge to improve society.

Although all of these founders responded to aspects of the social forces related to industrialization, their works are myriad and focus on a variety of subjects. Marx and Weber[1] are considered conflict theorists, Durkheim was a functionalist, and Mead and Addams were symbolic interactionists. However, to one degree or another, all of them looked at the roots of inequality in society and the possible solutions to this social problem. They used theories to explain how society works and how it might be improved. Like all explanations, some theories are more convincing than others. As you read through the chapter, think of which theories are most helpful to you as you try to understand how society operates and how you might work to make it better.

❖ KARL MARX

According to Marx (1818–1883), class conflict over the control of the production of goods leads to inequality in society. He maintained that in every economic age, there is a dominant class (the owners) that owns the means of production and exploits the other class (the workers). For example, in the feudal era, there were landowners and serfs, and in the industrial era, there were factory owners and factory workers. Marx believed that the workers would eventually overthrow the owners when

1. The economic means of production was technologically advanced enough so that it could easily support everyone in society

2. The workers united, realizing that they, as a class, were being exploited by the owners

Marx believed that the workers (proletariat) were under a "false consciousness" regarding their social class arrangements. That is, although they were conscious that there were class differences, they didn't understand why these differences existed, how those in power had manipulated the system to create these differences, or even the extent of these differences. Thus, although they *were* conscious of the differences in class, the understanding they had was a *false* consciousness. Marx believed that the owners (bourgeoisie) not only owned the means of production for market goods but also the means of the production of the *ideas* of society. In Marx's words,

> The ideas of the ruling class are in every epoch the ruling ideas, i.e. the class which is the ruling material force of society, is at the same time its ruling intellectual force. The class which has the means of material production at its disposal has control at the same time over the means of mental production, so that thereby, generally speaking, the ideas of those who lack the means of mental production are subject to it.[2]

This false consciousness prevented the workers from realizing that the capitalist system was designed to exploit, rather than benefit, them.

To counteract this false consciousness, Marx spent much of his life trying to unite the workers (proletariat), encouraging them to establish a "class consciousness," overthrow the ownership society, and transform the economic system from capitalism to communism. Consciousness was key to Marx's approach. As long as millions of individual workers saw themselves as struggling alone, or in competition with other workers, nothing would change. Marx wanted to impart a larger, societal view of the system to the poor, in which they would understand the role of the class system in their personal lives and act collectively against the system itself. His most famous attempt was *The Communist Manifesto* (1848), which concludes, "Let the ruling classes tremble at a Communist revolution. The proletarians have nothing to lose but their chains. They have a world to win. Workingmen of all countries, unite!"[3]

Conflict Theory is a modern extension of Marx's insights, although conflict theorists support democracy, not communism. In its general form, Conflict Theory begins with the assumption that at any point in time in any society, there will be different interest groups, different strata of society, and that much of what happens politically, socially, or economically is a manifestation of this conflict.

❖ MAX WEBER

Whereas Marx focused on class conflict and economic systems, Max Weber (1864–1920) looked more at the combination of economic and political power. Weber expanded Marx's idea of class into three dimensions of stratification: class (economic status—most important in capitalist societies), status (prestige—most important in traditional societies), and party (position in the bureaucratic structure—most important in advanced industrial, highly rational societies). In most eras, there would be a great deal of overlap between the three dimensions. For example, someone high in class would also tend to be high in status and political power. Unlike Marx, Weber was very pessimistic about attempts to eliminate inequality from society. He believed that even if one aspect of conflict and inequality could be eliminated, others would remain and perhaps become an even more important basis for inequality (e.g., the rise of the importance of difference in party position in the Soviet Union after status inequality had largely been eliminated). Weber's definition of power—"The chance of a man or a number of men to realize their own will in a communal action even against the resistance of others who are participating in the action"—remains the starting point for most modern sociological explorations of power relations.[4]

Weber's work on bureaucratic institutions helps us understand how power is won and held within advanced industrial societies of all types (whether capitalist, communist, or anything in between). Thanks to Weber, we now comprehend how powerful bureaucratic structures can be and how much of the structure remains intact even when the individuals in charge are replaced. For example, whoever controls the government bureaucracy in a highly developed nation can exert tremendous power over all aspects of that society. Controlling the government bureaucracy in society enables one to both control key institutions in society (including the military) and define the standards by which other bureaucracies will be created, evaluated, and carried forth. The crucial element of a power structure is its perceived "legitimacy." Because the power of lower-level functionaries depends on the same system that empowers those in higher positions, it becomes difficult and dangerous, and therefore unlikely, for someone in a lower stratum to really challenge the upper strata. The bureaucracy protects itself.

Bureaucratic structures are extremely efficient, whether they are being used well or poorly. One famous example of this is that the same highly efficient train system that existed in Germany before Hitler came to power (to transport workers and travelers) was used to transport men, women, and children to the death camps of the Third Reich. In fact, Hitler and the Nazis used the mechanisms of bureaucracy to carry out one of the most efficient (albeit horrible and incomprehensible) acts in human history.

Although Weber cautioned against the establishment of sociology as a science that should direct society, he did not shy away from using his knowledge to try to guide his country in turbulent times. Although pessimistic about the potential to eradicate inequality, he nonetheless felt obliged to do what he could to promote democracy in his society. His greatest impact on German society, as an engaged citizen, came toward the end of his life, during and right after World War I. He wrote many newspaper articles, memos to public officials, and papers against the annexationist policies of the German government during the war and advocated for a strong, democratically elected parliament and against the extreme ideologies of both the right and the left.[5]

❖ EMILE DURKHEIM

Whereas Karl Marx and Max Weber were conflict theorists, Emile Durkheim (1858–1917) adopted a functionalist perspective. According to this perspective, society is like a biological organism, with each organ dependent on the others for survival. Functionalists believe that society is made up of interdependent parts, each working for the good of the whole, rather than comprised of competing interests (as conflict theorists maintain). Durkheim believed that humans were selfish by nature and must be channeled and controlled through proper socialization by institutions in society. According to Durkheim, properly functioning institutions, such as the education system, family, occupational associations, and religion, will ensure that people work for the good of society, rather than just for themselves as individuals.

Seeing the political and social upheaval that plagued France during his lifetime, Durkheim studied how society operates and sought ways to make improvements. He argued that the existence of external inequality in an industrial society indicates that the socializing institutions are not functioning properly. Among his concerns were the problems of how to reduce inequalities and increase social consensus (solidarity). Durkheim used his various positions in the educational system to mold France's public schools around these ideas.

Durkheim divided inequalities into *internal* (based on people's natural abilities) and *external* (those forced upon people). Because society needs all its members doing what they do best in order for it to function most effectively, external inequality that prevents some people from fulfilling their innate talents damages all of society and should be eradicated. For example, if someone with the potential to find a cure for cancer—or just to be a good physician—never gets to fulfill this potential because she was raised in a poor neighborhood and attended a terrible school with teachers who never encouraged her to go to college, all of society suffers. Durkheim maintained that it was up to the various institutions in society to create opportunities for all society's members to become engaged citizens and share their gifts with the society.

❖ GEORGE HERBERT MEAD

George Herbert Mead (1863–1931), the founder of symbolic interactionism, was the first sociologist to focus on how the mind and the self are created through social processes. He was particularly influenced by how the human self develops through communicating with others via language and other symbolic behavior (symbolic interaction). According to Mead, humans are not truly human unless they interact with one another. In turn, the nature of our interactions with others determines how we see ourselves and our role in society.

Symbolic interactionists maintain that society is a social construction, continually created and recreated by humans. We may not realize it, but society is maintained by our implicit agreement to interact with one another in certain ways. As we "practice" certain patterns of interaction, we reinforce the belief system that society "just works that way." Therefore, by changing how we interact with one another, we can change society.

Mead used his sociological expertise about the influence of the social environment to contribute to several social programs and movements in Chicago. For example, he served as treasurer of Hull House, was a member of the progressive City Club, participated in a variety of local movements and social programs in the city, and edited the journal *Elementary School Teacher*. Mead also spoke publicly and often on behalf of the immigrants of Chicago, encouraging school reform to aid immigrants in the assimilation process.[6]

❖ JANE ADDAMS

Jane Addams (1860–1935) was both a sociologist and the cofounder of Hull House, an activist organization that advocated for women, racial and ethnic minorities, immigrants, the poor, and world peace. Widely recognized locally, nationally, and internationally, she rose to prominence in an era when few women were perceived as capable of public leadership. Recognition of Addams as a leader in the reform and peace movements culminated in 1931 when she became the first woman to receive the Nobel Peace Prize.

Addams worked closely with George Herbert Mead, on social issues concerning women and immigrant workers. Her sociological research in Chicago focused on issues related to the need for social reform, reducing inequality, and bridging the divide between the rich and poor. Addams (with her friend Ellen Gates Starr) founded Hull House in a poor, inner-city, immigrant neighborhood in Chicago in 1888, and it quickly became "an underground university for women activists focusing on questions of housing, sanitation, and public health."[7]

One of the more colorful Hull House studies involved researching garbage collection in Chicago. Lack of proper collection was spreading disease, particularly in poor, immigrant communities. In response, the Hull House Woman's Club stepped out of the roles expected of them as ladies in late 19th century Chicago and began to collect the garbage that was polluting the poor neighborhoods themselves! Before doing that, however, they used their sociological eyes and research skills to carry out

> a major investigation into the city's garbage collection system. Then Addams submitted to the city government her own bid to collect garbage. The resulting public uproar forced the mayor to appoint Addams as garbage inspector for her ward. The Hull House women formed a garbage patrol, getting up at 6 a.m. to follow the garbage trucks, mapping routes and dump sites, and making citizens arrests of landlords whose properties were a health hazard. Their vigilance moved garbage reform to the top of Chicago's civic agenda, forcing industry to take responsibility for its trash.[8]

Addams and the other Hull House residents were also responsible (to varying degrees) for a myriad of other social reforms, including the establishment of the juvenile justice system, women's suffrage, worker's rights, and child labor laws.[9]

The founders of sociology were deeply interested in using their knowledge for the good of society. One wonders how they might make sense of society today and what changes they would recommend to curb current systems of inequality. As we can see, their respective views of the world influenced how they perceived the social issues of the day and their proposed solutions for them.

Exercise 2.1   What Would the Founders of Sociology Say About. . . .

1. Consider some public issue of inequality today (e.g., the movement to privatize the world's water, the relaxation of U.S. environmental laws, the reduction of federal aid for college tuition, the high cost of running for public office, the decrease in funding for housing for poorer people, etc.).

2. Describe how each of the five founders of sociology discussed above might respond when told about these issues. Be sure that your answer also briefly summarizes what the issue is about.

3. Which of the responses makes the most sense to you? Why?

4. What is your own theory regarding the ability of individuals to act upon and create change within society? Do you pull elements from each of the above theorists in creating your own theory? Do you "start from scratch" and create something completely new? Compose an essay outlining your own personal social theory. Make sure to address the ability (or inability) of individuals to create change within their society.

Exercise 2.2	Going Deeper

As noted above, the founding theorists we discuss in this chapter were deeply influenced by the social problems that existed in their societies. Choose one of the theorists and obtain more information about his or her society. How did the social issues prevalent in his or her day influence his or her sociological perspective (theory) and research topics?

Now, return to the essay you developed above which outlines your own social theory. How do the social issues prevalent in your lifetime (as well as the values you've been socialized into) influence your sociological theory?

❖ THEORY AND SOCIETY

Sociologists use theory to elucidate and make sense of social patterns. Without theories, we would have little or no understanding of why society operates the way it does and how we might improve it. Looking at the world through a theoretical perspective can also help us detect patterns that we might otherwise overlook. For instance, conflict theorists are more likely to notice struggles for power, discrimination, and class inequality in society than are those who do not view society through a similar lens. Similarly, symbolic interactionists tend to be more aware of the impact of small group interactions and symbols. For example, symbolic interactionist theorists are quick to observe that seemingly minor behaviors (e.g., sitting with legs crossed or uncrossed) can have serious diplomatic repercussions.[10] Other theories can be useful in their own ways and, sometimes, as the Sociologist in Action section below illustrates, help us to achieve important practical goals. Theories can help us to make sense of the patterns we notice when we use our sociological eye. They can also help us to figure out where we should concentrate our focus.

Sociologist in Action: Brian J. Reed

Social Network theory helped the U.S. army to capture Saddam Hussein. Major Brian J. Reed, a doctoral candidate in the Sociology Department at the University of Maryland, College Park, used his sociological training in Social Network Analysis when he was stationed in Iraq and assigned the task to devise a strategy to capture the former Iraqi dictator. He described his use of Network Theory in locating Hussein in the following way:

The intelligence background and link diagrams that we built [to capture Hussein] were rooted in the concepts of network analysis. We constructed an elaborate product that traced the tribal and family linkages of Saddam Hussein, thereby allowing us to focus on certain individuals who may have had (or presently had) close ties to [him].[11]

Reed's expertise in network analysis allowed him and soldiers under his command to recreate and study a detailed picture of Hussein's social network, thereby determining where he would be most likely to hide.

Reed also maintains that his sociological training helped him to comprehend the Iraqi culture and, because of this understanding, more effectively carry out military operations in that country. Recognizing the practical applications of sociological research and theory, the Army Research Institute gave $1.1 million dollars in 2005 to The University of Maryland's Center for Research on Military Organization (CRMO), of which Reed is a member, to conduct research on social structure, social systems, and social networks.

As noted above, every theoretical perspective has its own view of society and tends to see patterns that the others miss. Some see the world from a wide-angle lens perspective, looking at larger (macro) social patterns (like functionalism and Conflict Theory) whereas others (such as Symbolic Interactionism) view society close-up, from a more detailed (micro) angle. It is important to remember that whenever persons use a particular theoretical lens (or any point of view), they will be more attuned to some social patterns than others.

Exercise 2.3   Different Perspectives Lead to Different News

This assignment will require you to watch the news for at least 3 hours a day for 1 week. It will also require you to have access to a wide range of stations. Watch CNN, BBC world news (now available in the U.S. on most cable networks), and Fox news, each for 1 hour a day for 1 week. As you are doing so, keep notes on (a) what stories they show on the news, (b) how they portray the news events (positively or negatively, for example), and (c) how they compare with one another. Pay attention to which stories are addressed by all three, and which stories are only covered on one of the news outlets. As you do so, complete the questions below.

Pick one news story that each network carries and answer the following questions.

1. How much time do CNN, BBC world news, and Fox news each give the story?

2. Are the events at the center of the story portrayed positively, negatively (or both) by, respectively, CNN, BBC world news, and Fox news? How do positive and negative portrayals differ from one another?

(Continued)

(Continued)

3. How would your knowledge of the news story be different if you watched just one of these news networks (CNN, BBC world news, or Fox news)?

4. How would your perception of the news story (whether the story was important, negative or positive, etc.) be different if you watched just one of these news networks (CNN, BBC world news, or Fox news)?

5. After the week is over, compare the different news stations' perspectives on the world. Were you able to clearly perceive three different perspectives? If so, how did they differ? Analyze, in detail, why it is that those differences exist. What does this tell you about the objectivity of news and news stories?

Exercise 2.4   Analysis of the News Media

Visit the Web sites of two national newspapers and one local paper. Some of the national papers you can use are the *New York Times* (www.nytimes .com), *The Washington Post* (www.washingtonpost.com), or *USA Today* (www .usatoday.com). A good place to search for your local paper is Hometown News (www.hometownnews.com).

1. What are the two or three lead stories in each paper? (Make sure that you are looking at all of them at approximately the same time on the same day.)

2. How similar are they in their editorial approaches? That is, to what extent do the different papers make similar decisions about which stories are most important and why (not visual similarities or layouts)?

3. Look at a couple of "inside" sections of all three papers, such as sports or entertainment. Repeat the comparison above by comparing the lead stories in each of those sections or the films or books chosen for review that day. How similar are the papers in these sections?

4. Optional: repeat the same observations for 5 consecutive days.

    a. Describe any patterns you have noticed.

    b. Now, repeat the same exercise using one conservative media source (such as WorldNetDaily at http://www.worldnetdaily.com/ or Intellectual Conservative at http://www.intellectualconservative .com/ or Free Republic at http://www.freerepublic.com) and one liberal source (such as Salon.com at http://salon.com/ or ZNet at http://www.zmag.org/weluser.htm or Online Journal at http://www.onlinejournal.com/).

c. Try the same exercise using one news magazine targeted toward women (such as *iVillage* at http://www.ivillage.com/ or *Women's eNews* at http://www.womensenews.org/index.cfm) and one toward the general public (such as *Newsweek* at http://www.msnbc.msn.com/id/3032542/site/newsweek/ or *Time* at http://www.time.com/time/).

Exercise 2.5   **Learning How Theory Is Applied**

Go to the book's Web site to find articles that use the theoretical perspectives discussed in this chapter.

Find one article for each of the respective theories and describe

1. the theoretical perspective that is used

2. how the author(s) use it

3. if either of the other two theories might also be helpful in making sense of the findings (and why or why not)

❖ DISCUSSION QUESTIONS

1. Given your answers to either Exercise 2.3 or Exercise 2.4, can you draw any conclusions about the perspectives that the different news sources adopt with regard to the social world? That is, do they tend towards a functionalist perspective, a Conflict Theory paradigm, a Symbolic Interactionist approach, or some other overarching worldview that affects the questions they tend to ask or the information on which they draw? Justify your answers.

2. Sociology has always been looked at a bit warily by leaders in most societies. Why do you think this might be? What about a sociological perspective might feel threatening to those in power and those benefiting from the current system?

3. Imagine you are a sociological theorist. What social issue would you choose to study first? Why? Which of the three primary sociological perspectives (Functionalism, Conflict Theory, or Symbolic Interaction) do you think you would use to explain your findings? Why?

4. If, as symbolic interactionists maintain, society is merely a social creation (that is created and recreated anew through our interactions with one another), why is it so hard to address social issues effectively? How might a symbolic interactionist respond to this question?

5. Which sociological perspective (conflict, functionalist, or symbolic interactionist) do you think is best able to explain inequality in the United States today? Why do you think so?

❖ SUGGESTIONS FOR SPECIFIC ACTIONS

1. Many sociologists note that sociological studies have pointed out good solutions to social issues but have been largely ignored by government leaders and the media. Go to the American Sociological Association Web page's "press room" site at http://www.asanet.org/page.ww?section=Press& name=Media or the Society for the Study of Social Problems Web site at http://www.sssp1.org/index.cfm/m/27/m/20.

2. Look around each Web site and find a study discussed on the site that provides a good basis for the use of sociological research in public policy. Write a letter to your school newspaper or another local paper describing the study and what you think would be a good public policy based on it. The following link from the Youth Ambassadors for Peace Web site will help you carry out this assignment: http://www.youthambassadors.com/resources/media.html.

Please go to our Web site at http://www.sagepub.com/korgen to find further civic engagement opportunities, resources, and peer-reviewed articles related to this chapter.

❖ ENDNOTES

1. Some consider Weber a functionalist.
2. Karl Marx [1845] 1963.

3. Marx, Karl and Friedrich Engels [1848] 1998.

4. Weber, 1946, quote in Gerth and Mills, p. 180.

5. Coser 1977, p. 242.

6. See the University of Chicago Centennial Catalogue's faculty Web page on Mead at http://www.lib.uchicago.edu/projects/centcat/centcats/fac/facch12_01.html. Accessed July 21, 2005.

7. Berger 1997.

8. Berger 1997.

9. See the Hull House Museum's Web site "About Jane Addams," available at http://www.uic.edu/jaddams/hull/newdesign/ja.html.

10. In Arab nations, it is regarded as impolite to cross one's legs. In India, it is impolite to show the bottom of your shoe, as you would by crossing one foot over your knee instead of your ankle.

11. Hougham 2005.

❖ REFERENCES

Berger, Rose Marie. 1997. "The Good Housekeeping Award: Women Heroes of Environmental Activism." *Sojourners* July/August 1997. Accessed at http://www.sojo.net/index.cfm?action=magazine.article&issue=soj9707 &article=970722 on July 22, 2005.

Coser, Lewis A. 1977. *Masters of Sociological Thought: Ideas in Historical and Social Context.* 2d ed. New York: Harcourt Brace Jovanovich College Publishers. P. 242.

Gerth, Hans and C. Wright Mills. 1958. *From Max Weber: Essays in Sociology.* New York, Oxford University Press.

Hougham, Victoria. 2005. "Sociological Skills Used in the Capture of Saddam Hussein." *Footnotes*, July/August: p. 3.

Hull House Museum's Web site "About Jane Addams." Available at http://www.uic.edu/jaddams/hull/newdesign/ja.html

Marx, Karl. [1845] 1963. *The German Ideology.* New York: International Publishers.

Marx, Karl and Friedrich Engels. [1848] 1998. *The Communist Manifesto.* London: Verso. P. 77.

The University of Chicago Centennial Catalogue's faculty Web page on Mead. Accessed at http://www.lib.uchicago.edu/projects/centcat/centcats/fac/facch12_01.html on July 21, 2005.

3

How Do We Know
What We Think We Know?

Sociological Methods

I n one memorable scene in the 1975 film *Monty Python and the Holy Grail*, in which a group of peasants drags a woman to the center of town to be burned at the stake, Sir Bedevere, the local lord, intervenes to be sure that justice is carried out.

Sir Bedevere: What makes you think she's a witch?

Peasant 3:   Well, she turned me into a newt.

Sir Bedevere: A newt?

Peasant 3:   [pause] . . . I got better.

Crowd: [shouts] Burn her anyway![1]

How much is revealed in this simple scene! First, this is the Dark Ages. (King Arthur, if he had actually existed, would have done his deeds in the mid-600's or so.) The Dark Ages were a time of superstition, uncertainty, and fear for many people. It was a time before

science, when religious spirituality contested with other spirituali-
ties and forms of magic to either shape or explain the world. Both
Christians and "pagans" believed that witches walked the earth and
that one must be on guard against them. Certainly, there were no
widely held assumptions about the nature of cause and effect or the
logic of demonstrating that one thing caused another. Evidence did not
need to be seen or examined; "proof" could come from the fact that a
lot of people agreed on something. "Burn her anyway" is a strong argument when shouted by a large crowd of people.

Finally, the scene is carried by the self-reflective totality of its logic.
That is, we start with a belief system, one that includes witches and
humans being transformed. We add an event: Someone claims to
believe that he was turned into something else. According to that perspective (common during the Dark Ages), that transformation must
have been caused by a witch. So a man thinks he was turned into
a newt, and those around him accuse someone of being a witch.
Challenged to support the claim (*she* is a witch), they resort to the orig-
inal definition of the event (there *is* a witch). Any evidence that worked
in her favor could, of course, reveal just how tricky those witches are.
There is no space in the argument to consider counter claims that she
is not a witch or that there are no witches. You might as well light the
fires. There is no way out of this logic.

Of course, things have changed a little in 14 centuries. Fewer people
believe in witches, most people have observed some kind of courtroom
drama, and science rests comfortably alongside religion and magic as a
widely accepted method of explaining the world. But scientific explanations rely on the logic of cause and effect, on the careful definition of
our terms and assumptions, and on the idea that evidence can be tested.
Even a casual observation of United States society suggests that these
concepts are not as widely understood or applied as we might hope.
For example, we might think we know that science has shown that the
Earth orbits the Sun, but how many people know how we know that?

Exercise 3.1   How Do You Know What You Know?

1. List five things about the contemporary world that you know to be true.

2. For each of the things on your list, identify the kind of fact you are listing:

   a. Basic definition (e.g., my house is at 123 NotReal Street)

   b. Name (e.g., Steve Nash was named the Most Valuable Player in the NBA in 2005)

c. Opinion (e.g., this class is more interesting than some other class)

d. "Established fact" (e.g., the world is round)

e. Testable claim (e.g., the percentage of Americans in the middle class has fallen over the past two decades)

3. Eliminate all of the facts in the first three categories and start again, until you have five established facts or testable claims. (Don't use any of our examples.)

4. For *three* of the five, find supporting evidence. Document your sources.

5. Using the evidence you found, write a brief paper demonstrating that the three facts are really true.

6. Write another page in which you discuss which facts were hardest or easiest to demonstrate, and why. Also describe whether you are more sure or less sure of your facts after having researched them.

Exercise 3.2   What Are They Talking About?

1. List five popular misconceptions about the world (see example below). That is, what sorts of things do people tend to believe are true even though they probably aren't true. For three of them, find some evidence that people think these misconceptions are true. It's not enough that one of your friends said something and someone else agreed. Find documentation that people actually have this belief. (Why only 3 of the 5? Because it's very hard to document what people really think.) For each of them, think about what sort of data would support the belief. Find some information that would contradict that. Example: (1) many people subscribe to the "gateway" theory of drug use: that "experimenting" with soft drugs leads one on a path toward addiction to hard drugs. (Marijuana is "soft;" cocaine and heroin are "hard.")

2. The Office of National Drug Control Strategy's Media Campaign includes a document of talking points for parents to use when discussing drugs with their kids. It includes a section on the gateway theory.

3. If the theory were correct, then there should be some data showing that a large percentage of people who had experimented with soft drugs when young later used hard drugs.

4. Estimates from the National Institutes of Drug Abuse (NIDA) suggest that the number of young people who have tried some drug is far, far

(Continued)

(Continued)

less than the number of adults addicted to hard drugs. So most of the early experimenters must not have progressed to harder drug use. But let's tread carefully here. Most people don't use any drugs. Among those who do, or have, most of the hard drug users did start out with some softer drug use. So there is a real relationship between the two. It just doesn't happen to be the relationship described by the gateway theory. We need a better theory to more accurately describe what the relationship is.

❖ THE THREE QUESTIONS

Before social scientists go public with their findings, they must establish the answers to three basic questions about their work: (a) How do you know? (b) So what? (Why is it important we know this?), and (c) Now what? (What do we do with this new information?). Let us consider each of these questions from the last to the first.

The "Now What?" Question

Research is the path toward answering questions. All of us can do research but it takes special skills to conduct social scientific studies. Research done by social scientists (and hard scientists) seeks to answer questions to which answers are not already known. If I am wondering whether there are any good movies on tonight, and I look up the schedule in the paper and find that there aren't, then I have answered my question. But I have not done social scientific research.[2] I might not know from day to day what is being broadcast, but that does not mean that this information is not known. So, social scientific research is a tool used to discover *new* findings.

By implication, someone has to have raised the questions first. Further, we like to assume that both the question and the answer are important and can influence society in some way. When we find the answer to our question, we should do something with that knowledge.

It has been popular to picture Newton "discovering" gravity as an apple fell on his head. It would be absurd to suggest that up to that point (mid-1600s, 1,000 years past the time of King Arthur) no one had noticed that things fall. But it is interesting to wonder how the observation (things fall) became a question (how and why do things fall). Something in the social, political or scientific world had changed so that it could become useful to answer these questions. Did things fall any differently after Newton had named the process? No. However, he discovered new information that powerfully influenced his and future societies when he answered the questions about why and how objects fall. His general theory of gravity changed the world.[3]

Your work does not have to change the way people view reality and the cosmos to have meaning. In the late 1950s, Harold Garfinkel attempted to explain the personal situation of a woman who had been born with male primary sexual characteristics (a penis) who in puberty had developed female secondary sexual characteristics (breasts) and who had to make a choice—accompanied by surgery—to define her sexual identity. Such cases are extremely rare and mostly unseen by the majority of our society.[4] One might think that sociologists would not be concerned with a single case. Yet, to appreciate and explain the case of "Agnes," Garfinkel had to address sexual norms, the power of "belonging," sanctions against deviance, and the strategies by which those with "abnormal" conditions may try to "cover" their conditions.[5] Agnes' biophysical condition combined with a vast and complex social world of meaning to create a problem that she had to solve. It was not, strictly speaking, the ambiguity of whether she was "really" male or female that defined the problem, but the social need for her to be unambiguous about it. This research raises questions about (a) the social categories within which personal identities and sexual identities are constructed, (b) how norms become normal and what happens when you violate them, and (c) how we define and use notions of what is or is not "natural."

Of course, once we have raised those questions, we have to start looking at everything that is considered natural or everything that is feared or hated because it is seen as unnatural. Very few people in this country are burned at the stake anymore, but hate crimes and vigilante assaults are not unknown. The usefulness of Garfinkel's research was not about Agnes. It was about what the rest of us think of Agnes and many other people and things that frighten or confuse us. Such research challenges us, both as individuals and as a society, to rethink our most comfortable and unquestioned assumptions about the world.

The "So What?" Question

A graduate professor advised his students that "we all want to contribute to grand theory, but also, we must eat." In other words, most research, most of the time, does not contribute to grand theory. Yet research is what sociologists do, and that is how scientific knowledge progresses. We take small steps, reviewing what is known about our interests, thinking about them in a new way or a new context, and testing the ideas that are generated by our thinking. When we prepare our research, we have to have some idea of what new knowledge we are after and why it is useful. The "so what?" question is like the "now what?" question. But where the last one asked why the world might need to know what we know, this question asks why sociologists need to study something.

Even abstract knowledge "for its own sake" is valuable in the quest to understand our lives, our world, and how those things interact. But, as we have noted in earlier chapters, sociologists have a social responsibility. Change happens all the time, all around us, and some of the consequences can be terrible in the long or short term. Where those consequences are obscured, it is our job to look for them. Where they are accepted due to public attitudes about who or what is valued, it is our job to identify and even question those values. Where the change is mostly good, we can learn from that as well.

Suppose we were to analyze every scene and underlying theme in *Monty Python and the Holy Grail*. (Both fans and academics have done so, though neither of the authors of this work has weighed in—yet.) How would we justify all of that effort on a 30-year-old movie by a defunct British comedy group? Shouldn't we be putting our time to better use, like examining political regimes, industrial shifts, or responses to natural disasters? Maybe. But there is still a lot to learn from and about popular culture. To answer the "so what" question, we do not need to show that lives hang in the balance. We need to show that there is something to be learned about our society or culture (or a different society or culture) that is worth knowing. If, for example, we concluded that Monty Python were a pretty funny bunch of guys, we would not be doing much. If, on the other hand, we concluded that Monty Python were popular and widely accepted when they were making fun of the British monarchy in general but less so when they were making fun of living members of the government, then we would be using popular culture to learn something about political culture.

The "How Do You Know?" Question

This is the big one, and most of the rest of the chapter will address this. To put it simply, however, we know that our findings are valid if we design scientific studies that are theoretically sound and driven by data. We ask questions, determine the kinds of data needed to answer them, figure out a plan for getting the data, and define a set of clear and consistent criteria for finding the answers in the data. Only then do we actually start collecting any data. We will explain each of those steps in further detail below.

We ask questions. Social scientific research is not carried out exactly like studies conducted in the natural or "hard" sciences.[6] We study things that are always changing, and always dependent on the time and place in which we are looking. A physicist can ask "What is the boiling point of water (at a given atmospheric pressure)?" A sociologist cannot ask "What is the boiling-over point of social unrest?" There isn't any such thing. Instead we have to ask "How does the occurrence of a single event of great injustice contribute to the likelihood that social unrest will lead to collective social action?" The answer is not a yes or a no or a number. It is a description of a social process in which some events lead to the possibility of other events. It's a probability estimate. But it is not a guess. We can show that our answers are reliable (consistent) and valid (accurate). Our questions are about how things work, and why they work as they do. And the best part is that no answer is ever final. There are always new circumstances, such as differences in history, culture, and geography, to take into account.

Once we have our questions, we have to figure out what data will answer those questions. If, for example, I wanted to know whether people in this country generally want lower taxes, I could conduct a national *survey* with a couple of tax questions on it. You have probably seen surveys. Most surveys are collections of short, simple questions on a set of related topics in which you choose your answer to each question from a short list of choices. Surveys allow researchers to collect a few basic measures of something from a very large number of people, in a short amount of time, and in exactly the same way. (If you collect data from some people one way and different people another way, it is not usually valid to treat the data as equivalent.) The answers given by any individual respondent (the person who responds to the questions) are not really important to us. What we really look at is the pattern of answers across hundreds, or hundreds of thousands, of cases.

Perhaps we already have reason to believe that people want lower taxes. So, now I might want to know what Americans are willing to give up for lower taxes (because lower taxes mean less government income and hence, usually, less government spending[7]). One might think this could be done with a survey, if we make the format more complicated. We can, for example, identify long lists of things that the government spends money on and ask people which ones they would be willing to spend less on if they could get lower taxes. But then, how do we choose the list? And if we ask "Which items would you trade?" how do we know that we aren't leading people to just identify the programs that they dislike, regardless of what they think about taxes? So just asking questions is not always the best way to find information.

Often researchers need to know more than just whether people do or do not approve of something. We need to know *why* they do or do not approve. We need to sit down and listen to people. This process is called an *interview*. Interviews involve asking people a series of *open-ended* questions on your topics and letting them answer in whatever way they like. The data are not the pattern of "yes" or "no" opinions, but the respondents' own words.

Interviews allow us to listen to and question respondents at length, and investigate intangibles like *why* they feel as they do. On a survey, I might ask you whether you think our nation should spend more or less than we do on loans to other nations. But how many people have any idea how much the nation already spends on that or what we spend it for? An interview gives more depth and more context than a survey, but it is longer, harder, and more expensive. Also, because you usually can interview far fewer people than you could survey, it's difficult to make good generalizations from interview data.

Surveys and interviews rely on *self-reported data*. That means that people tell us the answers. Yet, research and common sense both tell us that people do not always know why they feel or act as they do or how they will respond to certain circumstances. Few of us want to think of ourselves as people who will walk away from someone in need of help or cause harm just because we have been so instructed. If you ask people what they would do under circumstances in which strangers need help or in which their own actions cause harm, what will they tell you?[8] Sometimes you need to observe without asking.[9]

Experiments are one technique of observing how people will react to different conditions. In experimental research, the researcher measures the relationship between two variables by manipulating one of them and observing the other. If I want to know whether people will help a stranger in need, for example, I can create a situation in which someone appears to be in need of help. That's the *cause* part of a cause-and-effect relationship (the first variable). Then I can control circumstances so that a variety of people, one at a time, encounter the situation. Some of them will help, and others will not. That's the *effect* (the second variable). As much as possible, I would create a controlled environment in which almost nothing else can affect the outcome. For example, to control whether the subjects (the people being observed) were in a hurry or not, I might set up conditions in which they think they are waiting to meet with me, but know I won't be there for 10 minutes. That is, I can artificially create a situation in which they are not going anywhere while the experiment is running. The classic model of an experiment, which you have probably seen acted out in movies, involves a bunch of researchers (in white coats) in a lab, looking through a one-way mirror while subjects respond to different *stimuli* (the cause part).[10]

Fieldwork provides another way of measuring how people respond to stimuli. Fieldwork is, in some respects, the opposite of experimental research. Fieldwork requires the researcher to go out into the real world, where things are happening that we do not manipulate at all. The place where you choose to do your work is called your "field site." Field sites might include a park on a nice day, a campaign office during the course of a political campaign, spring training with a baseball team, an office, a courtroom, a classroom, or any other place where the kinds of activities in which you are interested happen. The researcher can not control, or really change at all, any of the many things that affect what people do. We can't create the stimulus. But, unlike in a laboratory setting, we can observe things as they actually occur in people's lives.

There are other techniques for data gathering and analysis, including the *content analysis* of the products of popular culture, mentioned above, and combinations of the techniques described here. For example, *focus groups*, or interviews conducted with a group of people, are a modification of interview techniques that incorporate some of the advantages of doing fieldwork.

Sociologist in Action: Johanna Foster

Informed by the sociological data that consistently show that access to higher education has the single greatest impact on reducing rates of recidivism, Johanna Foster decided to apply her academic training in feminist sociology to cofound two college-in-prison programs for incarcerated women in the greater New York City metropolitan area—one called *College Connections: Higher Education for Women in Prison* (with Gina Shea) and the other called *The Women's Reentry Initiative for Training and Education* (with Rebecca Sanford).

Prior to 1994, federal and state money supported higher education programs for incarcerated people. College-in-prison programs were numerous and accounted for a well-documented decrease in the rates of reincarceration. Today, higher education as a road to rehabilitation is almost entirely closed off for most of the 2 million people currently incarcerated in

(Continued)

(Continued)

the United States. For women prisoners, whose rate of incarceration has increased by more than 600% in the past three decades, the number of on-site college programs is dangerously small despite their proven effectiveness in reducing crime.

To help fill this gap in rehabilitation services, Foster obtained permission from administrators at a nearby state prison to conduct a needs assessment survey of the population to identify the interest in, eligibility for, and level of preparedness of women inmates for a nondegree, noncredit, college-bound educational program at that particular facility. Foster and her colleagues then used the findings from the needs assessment survey to persuade area educational institutions to matriculate students into what would eventually become a credit-bearing college program serving more than 150 women in that prison.

In another kind of applied sociology, Foster also teaches sociology and women's studies in the prison programs she has established, passing on C. Wright Mills' promise of the "sociological imagination" to students inside so that they can connect their "personal troubles" of incarceration to the "public issues" of race, class, and gender inequality. In doing so, Foster hopes to inspire student-inmates to use sociology themselves to understand their present circumstances and to improve their life chances once released.

Foster continues to conduct policy research on the state of higher education programming for women in prison nationwide, research that she most recently used to establish the NO GOING BACK Coalition for Incarcerated Women (NBGC), based in New Jersey. The NGBC regularly uses applied social research to educate a range of stakeholders about the importance of higher education and viable job training programs for incarcerated women and men alike. For more information, you can contact Johanna Foster via email at jfoster@monmouth.edu.

Statistical data gives us the big picture of trends and social changes. As you have just seen, we can use numbers to make connections between politics and the day-to-day realities of people who suffer from the effects of bad decisions. But it is great ethnographic fieldwork that really embraces the lived experiences of those whose lives and circumstances we study. (Ethnography refers to the study of cultural information, such as values and meanings, as opposed to data about structures, politics, and economics.) Eliot Liebow's classic 1967 study of an American ghetto, *Tally's Corner*, for example, was praised when it first appeared for the author's ability "to grasp the native's point of view" while emphasizing that "these 'natives' are other Americans; that their society is his society."[11] More recently, feminist sociologists have turned to ethnography[12] as a way of overcoming the cultural biases of research itself while conducting research on cultural biases.[13]

Exercise 3.3   Ethnography

1. Choose a public setting in which you can sit and take notes for at least an hour. The setting should be open to anyone and have lively social interaction. It must also be very unfamiliar for you so that you can experience it as an "outsider". Begin your observations by writing out a general description of your setting. Who is there and what are they doing? What sorts of activities go on in this place?

2. Describe how you fit into the setting. Are people noticing you doing your observations? What do you think people see you as?

3. For an intense 15 minute period, write down everything that you see happening. Try not to read anything into what you are observing. Observation notes might include things like: "two adults (1WM, 1WF)[14] walk in pushing a stroller with a very young child in it. They talk. The man goes to the counter while the woman takes a table. The man orders and purchases two drinks and brings them to the table." Notes should not incorporate a lot of interpretation. For example: "A couple with a child comes in. The husband asks his wife what she wants and then goes to get the drinks." You don't really know those things. You know the two people are adults, but you don't know their relationship or the details of their conversation.

4. After your notes are complete, try to make sense of them.
   a. What patterns of interactions did you see?
   b. What do you think they reveal?
   c. Why do you think that?
   d. What other explanations can you come up with?
   e. What would you need to observe or know in order to know which explanation was the most likely?

❖   THE THEORY PROBLEM

We recently saw a political survey sent out by a Senator to all of her constituents. Most of the questions asked respondents to rate certain proposals on a 5-point scale from "strongly disagree" through "disagree," "neutral," "agree," and "strongly agree." (This is called a

Likert scale, which is a common way to solicit political opinions.) But it was the questions that were remarkable. Many were of the form *"How do you feel about the federal government running up huge debts in order to . . . ?"*[15] The problem should be obvious. The question is so leading that the only acceptable answer is to disapprove. Yet the Senator will be completely within her rights to state that some overwhelming percentage of her constituents disapproves of whatever the issue is. However, although common in political and marketing research, creating the answers you want is not at all scientific or valid.

Social scientists guard against this sort of data abuse in many ways, but two particularly apply. The first is that we have to be open about our methods. We have to describe, in detail, where and how we get our data, including making our questions public. The second significant protection against misleading data interpretations is to define and describe clear and consistent criteria for data evaluation before you even collect your data. These criteria have to follow from our research questions.

Social scientists also have to indicate clearly the reliability and validity of our findings. We need to let our readers know, through a clear discussion of how we collected our data, just how sure we can be that our data accurately represent the population studied (validity) and whether or not we can expect that other researchers, using the same methods, would find similar results (reliability). Although not every study has to be high in both reliability and validity, we must clearly indicate just how valid and reliable our findings are. Unless we do so, information consumers will not be able to accurately judge the veracity of our findings.

Returning to the example of political policies, suppose we want to determine how popular or unpopular a set of policies are with voters. We would start by designing a set of procedures for measuring peoples' opinions. This might be in the form of a survey with a number of Likert scale questions on it (although not the questions from the survey we have seen). Recall that we had defined a five-point scale, in which answers 1 and 2 indicated disapproval, 3 was neutral, and ratings 4 and 5 indicated approval. In this case, the analysis is easy. When all of the answers are averaged, the number can be interpreted on the same scale: more than 3 indicates approval. Of course, real studies often involve much more complex criteria involving the interactions of many variables under different conditions. But the process necessarily involves first laying out the criteria by which the data will be used to answer the question, then collecting the data, and only then drawing conclusions.

Where do clear and consistent criteria come from? How can I say that it is reasonable to expect a particular outcome or pattern of behavior or odd to find something else? The answer, of course, is that our research is driven by theory. Sociological theory offers an array of ways for understanding and explaining the social world. Theories—tested notions of how and why people do things—lead to testable propositions about how and why specific sets of people would do particular things. Conflict Theory, for example, tells us that dominant groups will usually act in a great many consistent and predictable ways to maintain their dominance, including making claims about others' inherent inferiorities. Theories of gender and social roles in the United States tell us that men expect to have dominance in public roles, particularly those that involve the greatest amount of decision-making and money-making—areas that preserve and reproduce this advantage. The two together predict that men in leadership positions will routinely suggest that women are less capable of exercising leadership. Do they suggest that? That's a research question.

Exercise 3.4　Gender and Leadership

1. Write a 10-question survey about the differences between men and women. Let three of the questions deal with issues of leadership and decision-making. For each question, offer respondents the same three answers to choose from:

   Yes   No   I don't know

2. Survey 10 people, and summarize the results. Discuss what these results reveal.

3. Interview 3 people. Ask them the questions about leadership. But for each answer they give, ask them why they think so. Do not lead them to answer in any particular way. Just ask them to explain themselves, and let them say whatever they want. Write down their answers in as much detail as you can.

4. For each of your interviews, analyze the reasons people give for their beliefs.

   a. How often do they express their answers in terms of personal beliefs or personal experiences?

   b. How often do they express their answers in terms of anecdotes—stories that they might have heard about people they don't know?

(Continued)

(Continued)

    c. How often do they refer to fictional cases or characters, such as film or television characters, books, or other similar media?

    d. How often do they answer with reference to the example of a single real person whose life or circumstances are consistent with the respondent's belief?

    e. How else do people explain their beliefs?

5. What do the answers to these five questions tell you about how most people form their beliefs about how gender is related to leadership?

❖ DISCUSSION QUESTIONS

1. Political polls often ask potential voters whether they support or oppose something but rarely ask them whether they know much (or anything) about the topic. How do you think people with little or no knowledge of the topic come up with their answers to those questions?

2. Research has shown that when people are told that other people feel strongly about something, it influences the way in which they describe their own feelings about it. What does this finding suggest about major forms of research, such as self-reported data collection strategies?

3. What does this suggest about the effects of political advertising on elections?

4. Think of something that you and members of your family have long believed to be true. How would you test this belief? If your research led you to change your mind, how could you convince others in your family to reconsider their own assumptions on the issue?

❖ SUGGESTIONS FOR SPECIFIC ACTIONS

1. Find a Web site for an organization that advocates for or against something. Most advocacy organizations have Web sites these days, so you can start by choosing an issue about which people fight (e.g., legalized abortion, a flat tax, the death penalty), and then search out the groups that have positions on the issue.

Select a Web site used by one of the groups. Identify two or three major claims that they offer, on the Web site, in support of their position. Do they present real evidence to back up these claims? How well do they document their sources? Try to verify the data on your own. Also try to find contradictory information. Do you think they are being honest? What makes you think so? Create your own Web site (or alternate form of presentation) that describes the same issue in a more balanced way.

2. Research a policy decision recently made by your university. Ascertain how the policy was designed. In particular, determine what research was undertaken to determine if the new policy was necessary. Was the research done in a social scientific manner? Based on the research undertaken, do you think the university policy was clearly needed and well formulated? Write a letter to the editor of your school paper that describes your examination of the policy and the research that culminated in it. Be sure to include your evaluation of the research in your letter.

Please go to our Web site at http://www.sagepub.com/korgen to find further civic engagement opportunities, resources, and peer-reviewed articles related to this chapter.

❖ ENDNOTES

1. Dialogue found in The Internet Movie Database (http://www.IMDB.com).

2. Similarly, "researching" what is the best car to buy by reading consumer guides like *Consumer Reports* is not conducting true social scientific research.

3. *An Introduction to the History of Mathematics,* by H. Eves (1976).

4. See Sax 2002.

5. Garfinkel. 1967. *Studies in Ethnomethodology.* Englewood Cliffs, NJ: Prentice Hall.

6. Sociology, like psychology, anthropology, and political science, is a "social science." Physics, chemistry, and biology are "natural sciences," which study the physical world, or nature.

7. To simply borrow more money is a current popular alternative.

8. If you think you have an answer to that question, you are probably wrong. Some people will exaggerate one way; others will exaggerate the other way. Many will guess, and almost none will really know. But there will always be a lot of different answers if you ask a lot of different people.

9. Please note that observational research, like all research dealing with human subjects, must be approved by your school's Internal Review Board.

In almost all cases, you will need to obtain written approval from the people you plan to observe and provide assurances that no psychological or physical harm will come to them as a result of your research. See the book's Web site for more information about the ethics of social scientific research.

10. One of the authors of this book has a colleague who once had a job as a social researcher in a hospital setting. Even though they were doing normal sociology, conducting interviews, analyzing statistics, etc., everyone in the research group had white lab coats assigned to them to wear while they were in the hospital. The unstated point was that lab coats symbolized the authority of the researchers.

11. Rainwater, Lee. 1968. "Review of *Tally's Corner: A Study of Negro Street-Corner Men* by Elliot Liebow." *Social Forces* 46(3):431–32.

12. Many feminist researchers view traditional, social scientific, quantitative, research methods as constructed by men and influenced by a male-dominated view of society. Ethnography and other types of qualitative research, in contrast to quantitative work, tend to provide a more complete picture of and provide a greater voice for the individuals being observed.

13. Ribbons, Jane and Rosalind Edwards. 1997. *Feminist Dilemmas in Qualitative Research: Public Knowledge and Private Lives.* Thousand Oaks, CA: Sage.

14. Shorthand for "one White male, one White female."

15. This was not an actual question. We're exaggerating just a little to make the point.

❖ REFERENCES

Eves, Howard. 1976. *An Introduction to the History of Mathematics,* 4th ed. New York: Holt, Rinehart, and Winston.

Garfinkle, Harold. 1967. *Studies in Ethnomethodology.* Englewood Cliffs, NJ: Prentice Hall.

Rainwater, Lee. 1968. "Review of *Tally's Corner: A Study of Negro Street-Corner Men* by Elliot Liebow." *Social Forces* 46(3):431–32.

Ribbons, Jane and Rosalind Edwards. 1997. *Feminist Dilemmas in Qualitative Research: Public Knowledge and Private Lives.* Thousand Oaks, CA: Sage.

Sax, Leonard. 2002. "How Common Is Intersex? A Response to Anne Fansto-Sterling." *Journal of Sex Research* 39:174–79.

4

Creating Civic Engagement Versus Creating Apathy

Culture

Have you seen the *Sponge Bob Square Pants* episode when Sponge Bob goes to Sandy's house for the first time? If you have seen the show, you know that Sponge Bob is an underwater creature (a sponge) and Sandy is a squirrel (from Texas) who lives in an air-filled underwater structure. Sponge Bob did not appreciate the fact that he relied on water to survive until he stepped into Sandy's air-filled underwater home, couldn't breathe, became brittle, and started to disintegrate. Similarly, most people do not recognize how much they rely on their culture until they find themselves immersed in somebody else's.

Whether we are aware of it or not, we rely on culture for almost everything we do. All our decisions, from what clothes to wear, what to eat (and how to eat it), with whom we live, and what to do with our lives stem from our culture. Similarly, the languages we speak, the religions we follow, the sports team we root for, and our goals for what will make our lives "successful" are all given to us through our culture. Generally, sociologists divide the study of culture into the following three categories: (a) values, what members of society deem important;

(b) norms, the rules and expectations for behavior that guide people on how to act in society; and (c) artifacts (material culture), the tangible objects that people from a particular culture create. If values are what we believe in, what we want, and how we think our lives should be, norms are the set of rules we have established that govern how we can achieve those things we value. The values and norms that a society establishes will then influence which artifacts members of that society will develop and how they will make them.

Values and norms are social constructions, constantly created and recreated through interaction. That is, values and norms are produced by social processes, generally without plan, discussion, or decision. We just get used to doing things a certain way. Values are often debated, but there is no forum in which to "vote" on society's values. Therefore, they change over time and differ from society to society. Although there are some values that are shared by many societies (e.g., most capitalistic societies value hard work, money, and material possessions), values are not universal. For example, when a very physically fit person we know spent a year in a poor South Asian nation as a member of the Peace Corps, the villagers with whom she lived were constantly encouraging her to eat and gain some weight. The people there associated her thin figure with signs of poverty, a condition to be pitied. Meanwhile, back in the United States, she often experienced just the opposite reaction from people around her. Many people envied her physique and wished they could have a similar one! When one of us traveled to Lesotho, a small country in southern Africa, he was using a cane due to an injury. In Lesotho, he discovered that people who walk with canes are the most respected members of the society, those who have earned the cane through their wisdom. On his return to the United States, the author was quickly reminded that having a cane in our country is a sign of injury and weakness—a stark contrast to the admiration it brought to him while in Lesotho.

Likewise, social norms vary over time and from society to society. For example, in the contemporary United States, expected behaviors for men and women continue to change as new forms of interaction arise. Only a decade ago, it was commonly suggested that only desperate people used the Internet to find a date, but "singles bars" were popular. Today, as the ABC TV show *Hooking Up* exemplifies, arranging dates through Internet services is much more socially acceptable or "normal." According to a recent poll, more than half of all Americans believe they have an equal or better chance of meeting a romantic partner online than at a singles bar.[1] Where people go on their dates also varies from culture to culture. The first author remembers being rather startled as she took a stroll at dusk through a park in Cuernavaca,

Mexico to find *every* park bench filled with young couples. Most young couples there lacked the money to gain access to the private (or at least indoor) places many young couples go to on dates in the United States.

Girls and boys are also socialized differently in different cultures. For example, whereas girls from one culture are trained to hide their bodies, those from another are taught to flaunt their physiques. While writing these words, one of us looked out the window of her New Jersey home and saw several women get out of their car to look at the house that was for sale next door. It was a hot August day, but the women were completely covered by dark robes. The driver wore black leather gloves that extended far up her arms and only her eyes were uncovered. Although many other people had stopped to look at the house without drawing much attention from the author, her focus was (momentarily) diverted to this group of prospective buyers because of the clothing the women wore. Their manner of dress indicated that they were members of a subculture, meaning that they are a part of the larger U.S. society but also part of a smaller group within it that has its own norms, values, and customs.

Exercise 4.1	Student Survival Guide

Pretend one of your classmates is new to the United States.

1. Make a list of what he or she will need to know to survive. Make sure to include explanations about clothing, food, music, television, and everything that a non-American might need to know to "survive."

2. Once your list is complete, make a list of the norms and values that the items on your list represent.

3. Look at the list of norms and values and write a one-page essay analyzing what they tell us about American society.

4. Now, repeat this same exercise but pretend that you are writing it for a transfer student or an incoming first-year student to your campus.

❖ SUBCULTURES

To varying degrees, subcultures exist within dominant cultures (the culture upheld by the group that has the most power in a society). A subculture is a group of people with cultural patterns (values, norms, and artifacts) that distinguish them from the dominant culture. College students, firefighters, stay-at-home parents, first-generation Jamaican Americans, Mormon Americans, paraplegic athletes, White anti-racist activists, and working class Americans are some of the many examples of subcultures in the United States. Subcultures often arise around shared backgrounds. Italian Americans in an Italian enclave may form a subculture, whereas more "integrated" Italian Americans may not be a part of that group or may teeter between the subculture and the dominant culture. Subcultures also grow around shared activities. Surfers form one subculture, bikers another, and jugglers perhaps form a third. Yet sharing an activity is not enough to ensure the emergence of a subculture. There must also be times, places, activities, or habits that are shared by members of the group, and not by those in the dominant culture. There must be enough interaction for a common base of knowledge, habit, ritual, and meaning to develop.

For example, college students, as a group, tend to share certain values, norms, and artifacts that are different from those of people who are not enrolled in college. They may value high grades instead of big paychecks (perhaps as a means to get big paychecks in the future), tend not to sleep during the same time of day (or for the same number of hours) as most Americans, and create papers instead of handling or crafting material goods for purchase. They may also share patterns of leisure activity and home furnishing that are not seen elsewhere.

Although they have some noticeably different ways of thinking and behaving, members of subcultures share the same *guiding* values, norms, and artifacts of the dominant culture. The things they do and think that distinguish them do not threaten or work against the dominant values, norms, and artifacts of their society. For example, your classmates on the football team and your classmates who are members of the College Republicans may learn to think and behave in some different ways. Through doing so, each group creates its own subculture. However, the majority of both college football players and College Republicans follow the dominant norms and share the dominant values of the school and the larger society. Likewise, first-generation immigrant Jamaican Americans may enjoy different types of food than the majority of Americans and may tend to be a bit more family-oriented than Americans socialized only under the dominant American culture. However, both groups (albeit to varying extents) share and follow most of the primary values of U.S. culture (e.g., material success, progress, freedom, and hard work).

Members of subcultures both influence and are influenced by the dominant culture. For example, second-generation Jamaican Americans will tend to hold and follow more dominant American values and norms than their parents did. At the same time, the larger culture changes somewhat as immigrant groups interact with other members of society. The increasing variety of ethnic foods becoming common fare among Americans is a good example of how norms (in this case, what most Americans eat) change as the demographic makeup of the United States changes.

❖ COUNTERCULTURES

Groups of people who have cultural attributes that oppose those of the dominant culture are known as members of a counterculture. Such groups can be peace-loving, like the "flower children" of the 1960s, or willing to use violence, such as the Ku Klux Klan (KKK) and neo-Nazis. Members of countercultures often find it difficult to avoid violent confrontations, simply because they stand in direct opposition to some of the core values, norms, and artifacts of the dominant culture. The violence that erupted during the American Indian Movement (led by the group called AIM) of the early 1970s provides a good example of how the opposition of dominant and countercultural values and norms can lead to violent clashes. AIM (American Indian Movement) is a countercultural group with views that directly challenge many of the dominant U.S. values and norms, such as individual ownership of property and faith in the integrity of the U.S. justice and political systems. AIM's goals included a review of more than 300 treaties signed between Indian nations and the U.S. government (that the AIM leaders argued were broken by the U.S. government), autonomy for tribal governments, and a return to the traditional culture of the Indian nations. Many of the dominant U.S. values and norms (individual ownership of property, faith in the U.S. justice and political systems) were directly challenged by AIM. The U.S. government responded to this threat with powerful efforts to stop AIM by jailing leaders and surrounding protest enclaves with heavy weaponry, which resulted in several shootouts.

Those who challenge dominant cultural rules, beliefs, and values can face dramatic and harsh reactions by those who adhere to the dominant culture. For example, one member of AIM, Native American political activist Leonard Pelletier, was convicted and imprisoned for murder 30 years ago. However, he is widely believed to be innocent of the crime for which he was convicted.[2]

Some countercultures are extreme religious groups, cults, or other groups whose beliefs or goals place them in opposition to national laws. Such counterculture groups range from some fundamentalist Mormons[3] and evangelical Christians who believe in polygamy to radical Islamic groups such as Al Qaeda and extreme right-wing Christian Fundamentalists,[4] who use terrorism to promote their beliefs. All countercultural groups reject the dominant values, norms, and artifacts, seek out different ways of living, and (in some cases) try to impose their own culture against the will of the other members of society.

❖ RECOGNIZING CULTURAL PATTERNS

Now that we know what comprises a culture, we can begin to look for the patterns that help us to recognize the dominant norms, values, and artifacts of different cultures, subcultures, and countercultures. Members of almost any group of people who gather together on a regular basis create their own subculture. Think of your own groups of friends. You probably have ways of speaking to one another, in-jokes, and, perhaps, even modes of dress that set you apart, somewhat, from the rest of society. The same is true for the group of people who comprise your school's student body. Every campus has its own subculture(s). You have probably heard people talking about the "campus culture." What they are referring to are the values, norms, and artifacts that most people on your campus share that are often different from those found on other campuses or in the town in which your campus is located. Although we often speak of "the culture" of a community, it is clear that the various elements of the culture can contradict one another in the value systems or assumptions that they represent.

Every college or university has a reputation that is, in part, derived from the campus culture. For example, the first author received her undergraduate degree at a school known for its strong liberal arts education, Catholicism, heavy drinking among the student body, commitment to social justice, and ability to bring wealthy Catholics together to improve society and network effectively. The campus culture included valuing sports, competition, academic achievement, friendship, practicing the Catholic faith, working for social justice, and partying (not necessarily in that order). Some of the dominant norms were studying, playing sports, volunteering to help those in need, attending mass, hanging out with friends, hooking up (rather than dating), drinking lots of beer, and wearing J. Crew clothing (not necessarily in that order). The artifacts of the campus included finely manicured lawns (award winning, in fact), beautifully maintained old buildings (including chapels) in which to study, learn, and pray, cramped on-campus housing, run-down off-campus apartments to party in nearby, and

J. Crew clothing on almost every student on campus. These artifacts are more than just objects; they are manifestations of the values of the college. The finely manicured lawns, for instance, reflect a value of spending money on campus aesthetics rather than, for example, using some of that money to offer more scholarships to students from poor families.

Exercise 4.2 **Campus Culture: Seeing What's Around Us**

1. Think about your own campus. List five of the dominant values on your campus. Now list five dominant norms and five artifacts that reflect those values or which contradict those values.

2. Do you think your campus culture is different from or typical of most college campus cultures? How do you know this or why don't you know enough to answer this question?

3. Identify some of the visible subcultures on campus. What makes them a subculture, rather than just a bunch of people who have something in common?

4. Do you feel as though you are part of the dominant culture on campus? A subculture? A counterculture? All of these? Explain.

5. Why is a campus culture important? How does it influence how you spend your time and energy in college?

6. Do you think the campus culture has encouraged you to become a more active citizen? Are you engaged with activities on campus? Off campus? Why or why not?

❖ CAMPUS CULTURE AND CIVIC ENGAGEMENT

Studies examining the political culture in the United States reveal that most people are not politically engaged. Far less than half of the eligible electorate votes in most elections. Few know the issues for which candidates stand. Many do not even know the names of their elected officials. In a recent survey at one semi-competitive university, less than half of the students could name the Vice President of the United States. Only a handful of the hundreds surveyed could name one of their Senators. Less than a handful knew the name of their Representative. Political knowledge appears not to be valued and political participation is not the norm on that campus.

Nina Eliasoph, a sociologist and the author of *Avoiding Politics: How Americans Produce Apathy in Everyday Life,* provides some clues as to why so many Americans avoid civic engagement and why even those who volunteer their time to do good work avoid political conversations. Intensive participant observation of several volunteer and activist organizations led her to understand that our culture teaches us that political discussions and activism are divisive, fruitless, negative exercises that should be skirted, if at all possible. In her research, she looked for patterns in the behavior and conversations of members of several volunteer civic and recreational organizations to determine the dominant values and norms of the groups. However "civic" the groups might have been, they did not foster a culture in which members would discuss and debate issues of political significance. The few members of the groups who did bring up political topics of conversation in a "public" setting (in the group, rather than in private conversation) or who did suggest taking political action (other than the "normal" actions on the issues that the activist groups pursued) were discouraged from doing so. It appears to be a norm in American culture to make displays of consensus rather than broach important topics over which people might disagree.

The good news is that civic engagement does seem to be on the rise on college campuses. Student activism can be found on campuses across the nation. For example, by 2005, the "Boot the Bell" campaign, which demanded Taco Bell and its parent company Yum stop the practice of indentured servitude and increase the wages of tomato pickers, had spread to more than 300 college and university campuses when it ended in victory. Inspired by city initiatives to enact municipal "living wage" resolutions (e.g., Santa Monica, CA; San Jose, CA; St. Louis; Pine Bluff, AR; Boston; New York) and the successful 2005 student hunger strike in support of a living wage for workers at Georgetown University, college students are campaigning for living wages on campuses across the country. There are more than 200 United Students Against Sweatshops (USAS) campus chapters. Students at many schools (e.g., Florida State University, the University of Pennsylvania, the State University of New York, the University of Arizona, Duke University, and Georgetown) have forced their university administrators to stop buying apparel made in sweatshops and monitor the operation of the apparel factories (to prevent abuses of workers).

University administrative leaders also now realize the importance of teaching students how to effectively fulfill their obligations as citizens. Today, 144 state colleges and universities participate in the American Democracy Project, which focuses on providing service learning opportunities for students. More than 950 college and university presidents have signed the Campus Compact pledge to "educate citizens." Sociology students can use the tools of the discipline to be at the forefront of these efforts and make sure they are carried out in effective and just ways.

❖ DISCUSSION QUESTIONS

1. Can you recall a time when you gave discouraging feedback to someone who wanted you to engage in a conversation about politics or human rights? If not, why not? If so, why do you think you discouraged the person?

2. Can you recall a time when someone gave you discouraging feedback when you attempted to engage in a conversation about politics or human rights? If so, why do you think the person discouraged you? How did it make you feel? Importantly, how do you think you could have approached that conversation in a way that would have better been able to engage that person in a discussion about politics or human rights?

3. Do you think it's important to talk about political issues? Why or why not? If so, with whom?

4. How often do you talk to others about political issues? When you do so, with whom do you usually discuss them? Why? With whom do you usually avoid discussing them and why? Are you willing and able to discuss politics in a public setting or does it make you uncomfortable? Why?

5. Do you think political knowledge is valued on your campus? Provide an example to back up your answer.

6. Think about the dominant culture in the United States. What are some of the dominant norms, values, and artifacts that represent pride in civic engagement among Americans? Are any of them related to political participation? If so, how?

7. How do you know what your obligations are as a citizen? Who taught you what they are? How were you taught? When?

Sociologist in Action: Doug McAdams

Doug McAdams,[5] Professor of Sociology at Stanford University, used sociological research to figure out what compelled so many (predominantly White and middle class) northern college students to go to Mississippi to help register Black voters during the famous "Freedom Summer" of 1964. Of the 961 who applied to work as part of the Student Nonviolent Coordinating Committee's drive to register Black voters, the 720 who actually followed through and went to Mississippi (as compared to the 241 who did not) were much more likely to have had previous experience in civil rights activities and social activist organizations (many Church related) and connections to other Freedom Summer participants. These results indicate that those willing to risk their lives to register Black voters were part of a subculture with norms that supported social activism and efforts to support civil rights.

Exercise 4.3	Data Collection (for Dorm Dwellers)

Use participant observation to examine the political culture in your dorm.

1. Look at the list of organized events for one month (socials, lectures, etc.) as well as unorganized, spontaneous events, and attend as many of them as possible.

2. Try to participate in as many informal discussions as possible with your dorm mates during the same month.

3. At each gathering, carefully note the following:
   a. what type of gathering it is (friends studying together, watching a movie, gossiping about dates or, if it's a dorm event, the topic of the event, etc.)
   b. how many times political topics are raised (if at all)
   c. how many times political issues could have fit into the conversation but were not raised
   d. the reactions of others when political topics were raised: Did the person who raised them receive positive or negative feedback (sanctions)?

Exercise 4.4	Participant Observation of a Political Protest

Conduct a participant observation of a political protest or event on campus.

1. Find out what student activist groups (officially recognized or ad hoc) exist on campus by talking to other students, professors, campus activities, and so forth.

2. Choose an organization whose goals you feel comfortable supporting. Do not "infiltrate" a group by misrepresenting your own views.

3. Participate in organizing and carrying out at least one campus event or protest.

4. Throughout your time with the group, take note of how political issues are discussed in the group. Do they represent dominant culture, subculture, or countercultural values and norms?

5. What conversational topics are encouraged and what are discouraged (result in sanctions) in the group?

6. What are the reactions to the efforts of the group from fellow students, professors, professional staff, and administrators?

7. What do your answers to the questions above tell you about the norms and values of your campus culture?

Exercise 4.5	Environmental Values and United States Policy

Do dominant U.S. values about the environment match U.S. policy on the environment?

1. Go to http://www.publicagenda.org/

2. Pick an issue under the Issue Guide that you believe relates to a dominant value in U.S. culture.

3. Peruse the information available and write a paper that answers the following questions:

   a. What was the issue you chose to study and how does it relate to a dominant U.S. value?

   b. What were your own views on the issue before reading the site and how did you form your viewpoint on the issue (what aspects of your culture influenced your point of view)?

(Continued)

(Continued)

    c. Did your view on the issue change after reading the information on the site? Why or why not?

    d. Recommend several practical suggestions for working for change on the issue. Include a discussion of what can be done on your campus to work for change and what you can personally do.

Exercise 4.6	Globalization: The Great Cultural Divider?

In an August 2004 editorial in *The New York Times*,[6] columnist David Brooks argued that globalization, rather than leading to cultural homogenization, as some feared, has actually fostered increased cultural segmentation, division, and conflict. In his words,

> Not long ago, people said that globalization and the revolution in communications technology would bring us all together. But the opposite is true. People are taking advantage of freedom and technology to create new groups and cultural zones. Old national identities and behavior patterns are proving surprisingly durable. People are moving into self-segregating communities with people like themselves, and building invisible and sometimes visible barriers to keep strangers out.
>
> If you look just around the United States you find amazing cultural segmentation. We in America have been "globalized" (meaning economically integrated) for centuries, and yet far from converging into some homogeneous culture, we are actually diverging into lifestyle segments. The music, news, magazine and television markets have all segmented, so there are fewer cultural unifiers like *Life* magazine or Walter Cronkite.
>
> Forty million Americans move every year, and they generally move in with people like themselves, so as the late James Chapin used to say, every place becomes more like itself. Crunchy places like Boulder attract crunchy types and become crunchier. Conservative places like suburban Georgia attract conservatives and become more so. Not long ago, many people worked on farms or in factories, so they had similar lifestyles. But now the economy rewards specialization, so workplaces and lifestyles diverge. The military and civilian cultures diverge. In the political world, Democrats and Republicans seem to live on different planets.

From Brooks, David, "All Cultures Are Not Equal," in *New York Times,* August 11, p. A23. Copyright © 2005, The New York Times Company. Reprinted with permission.

1. Do you agree with Brooks that U.S. citizens are increasingly separating into distinct and isolated subcultures? Do you think that this trend could lead (or has led) to more countercultures in the United States?

2. Write a one-page outline of how you would carry out research to test one (or more) of David Brooks' statements in the passage above.

❖ SUGGESTIONS FOR SPECIFIC ACTIONS

1. Brainstorm with two or three of your classmates as to how you might promote civic engagement within the existing campus subculture. If you do not think it is possible to do this within the existing subculture, how might you change the subculture to promote civic engagement on campus? Act upon these ideas.

2. Organize a campus debate about a civic issue that affects the life chances of students on campus. Analyze the campus culture to figure out how to most effectively promote and advertise the event (and do so!).

3. Conduct three focus groups (after obtaining proper Internal Review Board approval) that explore how your fellow students define (a) the ideal campus culture and (b) the actual dominant norms and values of the campus culture. Recruit interested members of the focus group to come up with an action plan to disseminate and act on your findings.

Please go to our Web site at http://www.sagepub.com/korgen to find further civic engagement opportunities, resources, and peer-reviewed articles related to this chapter.

❖ ENDNOTES

1. IPSO News Center: Research, Opinion & Insights 2002.

2. Two of the most well-known books that supply information about the Pelletier case are Jim Messerschmidt's *The Trial of Leonard Peltier* and Peter Matthiessen's *In the Spirit of Crazy Horse*.

3. The Church of Jesus Christ of Latter-Day Saints banned polygamy in 1890.

4. Like Eric Robert Rudolf, who carried out the 1996 Centennial Olympic Park Bombing and other bombings that targeted gay and lesbian Americans and abortion clinics.

5. McAdams 1988.

6. Brooks 2005.

❖ REFERENCES

Brooks, David. 2005. "All Cultures Are Not Equal." *New York Times*, August 11, p. A23.

Eliasoph, Nina. 1998. *Avoiding Politics: How Americans Produce Apathy in Everyday Life*. Cambridge: Cambridge University Press.

IPSO News Center: Research, Opinion & Insights. 2002. "Move Over Single's Bars, Online Dating Taking Hold." Accessed at http://www.ipsos na.com/news/pressrelease.cfm?id=1635 on August 19, 2005.

Matthiessen, Peter. [1983] 1992. *In the Spirit of Crazy Horse*. New York: Viking Press.

McAdams, Doug. 1988. *Freedom Summer*. New York: Oxford University Press.

Messerschmidt, Jim. 1983. *The Trial of Leonard Peltier*. Boston: South End Press.

5

Learning How to
Act in Society

Socialization

W ould you like to make someone smile? Smile at them! It's almost impossible not to smile back when someone is smiling at you. A smile is one of the first symbols we learn to use to communicate with others.

Babies learn to smile by interacting with their caregivers who (often) smile at them as they play with, change, and feed them.[1] They quickly learn that smiling can make their parents happy (and, in particular, happy with them). The first author's second daughter learned this trick, to great effect, when she was an infant. She could even get her exhausted parents to smile while changing her at 3:00 a.m. After fumbling their way to the changing table, they would look down to see her beaming at them with a big grin. Even those *very* sleep-deprived people couldn't resist their urge to smile back at the baby who had just awoken them from their slumber. How could they not—she looked so happy to see them!

On a more somber note about learned behavior: Have you heard the tragic story of Isabelle, a girl who was kept locked in a closet until she was 6 years old?[2] When she was finally released, her behavior was like that of an animal. She didn't know how to speak, eat with utensils, use a toilet, or even smile. Her lack of interaction with other humans had prevented her from going through a process of socialization, the way in which we learn how to interact effectively in society. Isabelle's experience (and that of other children deprived of social interaction) indicates that human contact and social interaction is crucial for proper human development.

❖ THE LOOKING GLASS SELF

Everyone around us influences our self-perception and our behavior in some way. The early symbolic interactionist Charles Horton Cooley described how others affect our self-image with the term the "Looking-Glass Self."[3] By this, he meant that we perceive ourselves based on how we *think* others see us. For instance, one of the authors of this book often finds himself experiencing the Looking Glass Self when teaching a class. It is part of the job of a professor to continuously discern whether or not students understand a lecture and are engaged with the subject matter. Often, when the author looks out toward the class and sees blank expressions, he assumes that this means that the class does not understand what he is saying. He reacts to this by re-explaining the concept and trying to find a new way to present it. But what if the students are exhibiting the blank expressions because the concept was simple and the professor has already spent too much time on it? (Or what if they look that way because this is how they look when they are watching television, and they have blurred the difference between a recorded broadcast and a live interaction?) What Cooley's Looking Glass Self demonstrates is that our actions and behaviors are reactions to our *interpretations* of the people, objects, and situations we encounter. What matters in the above scenario is *not* what the students are actually thinking, but what the professor thinks they are thinking. This social-izes him into his subsequent behaviors, in this case reiterating a concept that the students already understood! Cooley's theory can best be summed up as such: "I am not what I think I am and I am not what you think I am. I am what I think you think I am."

❖ THE GENERALIZED OTHER

George Herbert Mead established a theory of social behaviorism to show how individuals' personalities are developed through social experience. According to Mead, we develop a self (the part of our personality that is a combination of self-image and self-awareness) through (a) interacting with others through the use of symbols and (b) being able to see ourselves through the perspective of others. Eventually, through social interaction, we complete our creation of the social self by developing a sense of how we might be seen through the eyes of any person (the "generalized other") who espouses the prevailing norms and values of the society in which we live. We find ourselves watching and judging our own actions through the eyes of this generalized other, even when no other is present. Eventually, we internalize the awareness of how our behaviors *seem* socially. Our personal identities, therefore, contain our sense of who we are in society. No self can develop without social interaction.[4]

❖ THE ID, THE EGO, AND THE SUPEREGO

Sigmund Freud developed a theory of personality in the early 1900s that has influenced almost all studies of human personalities since then. A crucial part of his work was to explore the role of the *unconscious* in human identity and behavior. He broke down the unconscious into three sections, the id, the superego, and the ego. According to Freud, the *id* consists of people's innate desires and urges (which are primarily centered on instant gratification, sex, and violence). The *superego* is the part of our unconscious that has internalized the dominant norms and mores of society (particularly what comprises "right" and "wrong" behavior). The superego represents our awareness of others, particularly of their reactions to ourselves. The *ego* works to balance the desires of the id with the moral impulses of the superego. The ego is the part of the self with which we choose to act or not act on our desires. For Freud, the ego is constantly testing our sense of what we want against our sense of what is expected of us. We learn about the dominant norms of society and how to balance them with our innate desires through socialization with other human beings.

❖ PRIMARY SOCIALIZING AGENTS

Of course, some people make more of an impact on us than others. These people tend to comprise or come from one or more of the primary socialization agents in our society. Today, in the United States, there are five primary socializing agents: family, peers, education, the media, and religion.

Family

We cannot choose our parents, but they do have a tremendous influence over who we become. For most of us, from the moment we are born, our family members, particularly our parents, are those with whom we interact first and for the most amount of time. Whether a parent constantly tells us that we are mean and stupid or repeatedly praises us for being so caring and brilliant (or anything in between) can largely determine how we view ourselves (dumb or smart) and how we behave (mean or kindly). These lessons of socialization can influence what we become. For example, we are much more likely to put energy into our work if we believe we are smart and capable than if we thought we were neither bright nor professionally competent.

Socialization also teaches us what we want (values) and helps to give us a roadmap to achieve these things (norms). We are not *born* as Americans or Christians or Italians or Republicans or . . . fill in the blank. We *become* these things because our families and other socializing agents have socialized us into becoming these things. Parents from different societies (with different values and norms) socialize their children in different ways. For example, parents in the United States are likely to teach their children to desire different things than would parents in other societies, such as those in Afghanistan, El Salvador, or even Canada.

Families also influence how we behave as public citizens. For example, young adults are twice as likely to vote if they have parents who (a) discuss politics and (b) vote themselves.[5] Engaged parents often shape engaged young Americans.

Exercise 5.1	Family Influence and Civic Engagement

Think about how your family has influenced your level of civic engagement.

1. Did your parents and other family members discuss political issues with each other when they were around you (at the dinner table, over coffee, etc.)?

2. Did your parents and other family members discuss political issues with you when you were growing up? Do you discuss political issues with them now? Why or why not?

3. If yes, have they asked you to participate in political activities with them? Have you? If so, in what ways? How did those experiences influence your own view of the importance of civic engagement?

4. If your parents and other family members are not active citizens, why do you think they are not? What do you think might make them become active?

5. Overall, how do you think your parents' and other family members' level of civic engagement has affected your own activism? Taking a moment to really evaluate the implications of this, how do you feel about your own level of activism and how you socialize your own children (or how you will when or if you have kids)?

Peers

Our peers also have a great effect on how we view ourselves, how we interact with others, and what we become. Who hasn't wanted to impress their friends and who hasn't at some point or other taken on some of the values and norms of their peer group? As soon as we are able to interact with people outside of our family, we begin to be influenced by peers (those similar to us in terms of age, social class, etc.). The children you played with in your neighborhood, school, sports teams, and so forth comprised your peer group as you were growing up. To varying degrees, our peers influence our self-perception and behavior in the same way our family does. It is through our associations with others who are "like us," our *peer reference group,* that we learn what people like us are like.

One Web site for a summer camp includes a quote from a camper saying "At school I'm a nerd, but here I'm cool."[6] You have probably heard other stories of people growing up with two different peer groups (for instance, one that consists of classmates during the school year and campmates or children in the area where one vacations during the summer). We are aware of one story of a young man who remembers being perceived (and thinking of himself) as a cool kid and a jock when around summer friends and as a lonely loser when among school peers. As a result, he found himself acting out the roles attributed to him by the different groups. He kept to himself and was rather shy and aloof with his classmates but found himself leading his summer friends on wild adventures he never would have dreamed of pursuing during the school year. His self-perception actually became a self-fulfilling prophecy. He changed his behavior from one environment to the other to become the person he thought his peers saw. This young man's story is a great illustration of "The Looking Glass Self."

Both his self-perception and his behavior were strongly influenced by how he imagined his peers viewed him.

When the first author interviewed people who have both a Black and a White parent for an earlier book project, she found that even people's racial identity could be influenced by how they think others view them. Phillip, a biracial young man whose racial features did not clearly indicate his racial background, adapted his racial identity to avoid getting beat up in some of the rough neighborhoods in which he grew up. He described how his experience in a Puerto Rican and Black inner-city neighborhood influenced his racial identity in the following way:

> I got beat up by [some] black kids for being half-white. I started saying, "No, no, no. I'm Puerto Rican. I'm Puerto Rican. I'm Puerto Rican." And then, next thing I know, it's all cool because of the fact that my uncle married a Puerto Rican woman. Another uncle of mine married a Puerto Rican. So that's two different sets of interbreeding and families, Puerto Rican, blacks, till it's all Puerto Rican. . . . I'm Puerto Rican.

Not only did Phillip change his declaration of racial identity, he actually began to believe that he was Puerto Rican instead of Black and White. Supported by his Puerto Rican relatives and his ambiguous racial features, Phillip became Puerto Rican.[7]

Exercise 5.2	Your Many Selves

Everyone acts (at least somewhat) differently among different groups of people. Write a one-page essay describing different situations in your life in which you act almost like you are different people.

Exercise 5.3	Friendships and Civic Engagement

Think about how your peers have influenced your level of civic engagement.

1. Do your peers discuss political issues with each other when they are around you?

2. Did your peers discuss political issues with you when you were growing up? Do you discuss political issues with your peers now? Why or why not?

3. Do your peers vote? Have you ever gone to the polls with a peer? If so, what was that like?

4. Are your peers civically active? If yes, in what ways? If yes, have they asked you to participate with them? Have you? If so, in what ways? How did those experiences influence your own view of the importance of civic engagement? If your peers are not active citizens, why do you think they are not? What do you think might make them become active?

5. Overall, how do you think your peers' level of civic engagement has affected your own activism? Taking a moment to really evaluate the implications of this, how do you feel about your own level of activism and how might you socialize your own children when or if you have kids?

Education

Institutions have multiple roles. Our educational experiences play a major, often somewhat hidden, role in our socialization process. Schools serve the primary purposes of giving us the tools we will need to operate in society and socializing us to adapt and follow the values that society has deemed most important. One of the goals of schools is to teach Americans a "hidden curriculum": to respect the rules of how our society operates, to not challenge the status quo, and to act in nondisruptive ways. For example, among the first things you learn in school are how to raise your hand, wait your turn, sit quietly, and follow directions. Many of these habits are useful skills that kids need to learn to interact with other people. Yet these same practices also reveal the school's need for children to be disciplined so that they can be managed in large numbers.

School also teaches you the basic values and beliefs of our dominant culture (as outlined in Chapter 4). What we learn about different racial, ethnic, gender, and social class groups through our schools and textbooks influences how we perceive and judge these groups throughout our lives. It also helps us understand our own social status and role in society.

Dominant (or popular) values and beliefs determine, to a great extent, what is taught in our schools at any given time. It is important to remember that history is taught through the perspective of the dominant groups in our society. An examination of how the portrayal of

U.S. history has changed over the years (as different racial–ethnic groups gain power in the United States) is a good illustration of this fact.

Exercise 5.4   **The Hidden Curriculum: History, Values, and Socialization**

Find a U.S. history book currently used at a local school.

1. Note the title of the book. What image does the title convey?

2. Look at the table of contents. What topics are covered? Think of five additional chapters you think could or should have been included in the book. Why do you think they could or should have been included? Why do you think they were not included? What do your results tell you, sociologically, about the values that our curriculum deems most important? Besides the need to keep textbooks a certain length, why else do you think that certain topics are not included?

3. Compare how different racial, ethnic, gender, and social class groups are covered (or not covered) in the book.

4. Compare the Civil War chapter in the history book you obtained with Howard Zinn's chapter on the Civil War in his book, *A People's History of the United States, 1492–present* (New York: HarperCollins 2003)—your school library should have a copy. What are the similarities? What are the differences? How do you think the differences relate to the "hidden curriculum" of the public school system in the United States?

5. How do you think members of different races and ethnicities, genders, and social classes would view their respective status positions and roles in society after reading each of the chapters?

Media

The *media* refers to any widespread dissemination of information. Among the various media outlets, television is arguably the most important socializing agent. Children in the United States watch an average of 4 hours of television a day. During those viewing hours, they are exposed to shows created by corporations to draw viewers to the advertisements they use to market their products before, during, and after the programs. Their perspective of the world, therefore, is influenced to a considerable extent by a carefully selected set of images (in both the television shows and the advertisements) used to promote business for advertisers. Accurate or not, television shows are one of the major windows many Americans have on the world around them. In a nation increasingly segregated by social class, TV shows are often the only way that some Americans are exposed to other groups of Americans. Our perceptions of different age, gender, racial, ethnic, and other groups, and our images of ourselves (remember The Looking Glass Self), are influenced by the way these groups are portrayed in the media.

Exercise 5.5	Content Analysis of Television News Programs

For this assignment, you are to conduct a content analysis of 10 news programs.

Make 10 copies of the Content Coding Sheet (Figure 5.1, top). You will fill these charts in as you view your news programs. As you fill out these charts, there are a few rules:

1. You must view news programs at the same time slots (e.g., early morning, midmorning, afternoon, prime time, late night).

2. You must try to view the same types of news programs (e.g., local or national and international [ABC, NBC, Fox News, CBS, PBS, BBC])

3. After having filled out your Content Coding Sheets, you will then fill out your Data Summary Sheet (Figure 5.1, bottom). This will give you overall numbers and percentages.

4. Once you have completed the data collection, join with three other members of your class to analyze your collective data. What do your results tell you about how social activism is portrayed on the news programs you examined? What does this tell you about how we are socialized to view social activists and social activism?

Religion

Americans are, overall, much more religious than citizens of other wealthy nations (e.g., the numbers of Evangelical Christian and Muslim Americans are increasing). Americans are twice as likely as Canadians and more than twice as likely as Japanese and Western Europeans to say that religion is "very important" to them.[8] Those who attend religious services and read religious writings are exposed to

Figure 5.1   Content Coding and Data Summary Sheet

Content Coding Sheet

Type of social activism: _____

Name of news program: _____

Station viewed on (provide channel and network): _____

Local or national/international: _____

Time of day: a.m.   p.m.

Note the number of examples of social activism covered and note the type—for example, (a) violent or peaceful, (b) disruptive or nondisruptive—and how it is portrayed (positively or negatively) by checking under the appropriate columns.

Examples of Activism	Violent	Peaceful	Disruptive	Nondisruptive	Portrayed Positively	Portrayed Negatively
1						
2						
3						
4						
5						

Data Summary Sheet

News program: _____

Station/network: _____

Local or national/international: _____

Time of day: _____

Type of Activism	Number Portrayed Positively	Number Portrayed Negatively
Violent		
Peaceful		
Disruptive		
Nondisruptive		
Total		

teachings about certain ways to view and act in the world that influence how they view themselves and interact with others. For example, many of the student activists who participated in the Civil Rights "Freedom Summer" did so because they were motivated by the Christian ethic of brotherly love they learned from attending religious services and participating in religious organizations.[9]

❖ DISCUSSION QUESTIONS

1. How do you think we can create a society in which citizens are socialized to become knowledgeable and effective participants?

2. In what ways did your socialization through each of the five primary socializing agents (family, peers, education, media, and religion) encourage you to become an engaged member of society? In what ways did each discourage you from becoming an engaged member of society?

3. How might the world be different if our primary socializing agents fostered civic engagement among citizens?

4. What might happen if only one or two primary socializing agents encouraged civic engagement among citizens? Which do you think need to do so, in order to effectively foster civic engagement across the United States?

5. What worldwide socializing agents might effectively encourage civic engagement across the globe?

Sociologist in Action: Susan Ostrander

Colleges and universities are socializing agents capable of educating citizens and strengthening democracy. However, many campus leaders are unsure of how to encourage civic engagement in ways that will benefit the campus and the community, while adding to intellectual knowledge. Tufts University Professor Susan Ostrander used her sociological skills to find ways universities can achieve these goals.

Ostrander's work is a great example of how sociologists can connect the sociological eye (looking beneath the surface to understand how society works) and social activism (*using* that sociological knowledge to make society better). In 2001, partly as a means of finding useful information to

(Continued)

(Continued)

set the direction for Tufts' new University College for Citizenship and Public Service, Ostrander studied five campuses around the United States known for excellence in civic engagement. Drawing on data gathered during intensive 2-day site visits to each campus, Ostrander concluded that (a) student learning, community benefits, and knowledge creation—contrary to efforts to develop universal best practices—occur in dynamic and changing relationships to one another; (b) sustained faculty involvement requires an intellectual rationale for campus engagement connected to well-defined scholarly projects; and (c) successful engagement by higher education requires new organizational structures that create campus–community partnerships in which power is truly shared.

Ostrander uses her findings in her classes. For example, she regularly arranges opportunities for students to work with local community organizations on issues related to her course "Wealth, Poverty, and Inequality." Ostrander has worked with her students in her course "Social Change and Community Organizing" to survey residents of public housing about their involvement in their own community and the issues that most concerned them. This research provided the basis for community organizing at the housing development. Ostrander and her students also partnered with a local immigrant rights organization to initiate a project aimed at empowering local teens to urge their high school to provide more guidance programming for low-income students who may be eligible for college.

Ostrander's ability to connect the classroom to the community enables her students to fulfill the two core commitments of sociology: They are learning how society works and using that knowledge in efforts to make it better.

❖ SUGGESTIONS FOR SPECIFIC ACTIONS

1. Determine whether or not your college or university has committed itself to the educating citizens movement and whether it has taken steps to teach its students to become knowledgeable, effective citizens. One way to do this would be to find out if your President or Provost has signed the Campus Compact pledge (found at www.campuscompact.org), joined the American Democracy Project (http://www.aascu.org/programs/adp/about/default.htm) or some other such initiative to promote civic engagement in higher education. If he or she has, compare the goals of the initiative with the results you

see on campus. Write a letter to your Provost or President and your school newspaper that includes the results of your research. If your school has not embarked on such a mission, write a letter to your Provost or President that explains what the educating citizens movement is about (after having looked at the Campus Compact and Democracy Projects Web sites) and inquires as to what steps your school has taken to educate well-informed and effective citizens.

2. Explore the institutionalized connections your college or university has established with the surrounding community (e.g., service-learning courses, school sponsored community centers, school sponsored tutorial programs, research partnerships between professors and community members, etc.) and write a letter that summarizes your key findings to your local paper (to help inform the campus community about these matters).

3. Participate in one of the events your university uses to connect to the local community (whether it be sponsoring a community fair, volunteering to work in a soup kitchen or a local school, etc.). Use your sociological eye to examine the power dynamics behind how the event or program is coordinated through the school and community. For example, who designed the program (school or community or both)? Who coordinates the program (school or community or both)? Who has authority over the program (school or community or both)? Who funds the program (school or community or both)? How do you think this type of coordination influences the overall program?

4. Set up an interview with the person who coordinates the orientation program for first year students at your university. Inquire as to (a) how orientation socializes students into successfully learning and adopting the campus rules, norms, and values and (b) what mechanisms are used during the orientation process to socialize new students into the role of educated and engaged citizens. If no such mechanisms are currently practiced, make some suggestions about what could be put into place to the person who coordinated the first-year orientation program.

Please go to our Web site at http://www.sagepub.com/korgen to find further civic engagement opportunities, resources, and peer-reviewed articles related to this chapter.

❖ ENDNOTES

1. For more information about the development of smiles in babies see "The Development of Anticipatory Smiling," by Meaghan Venezia, Daniel S. Messinger, Danielle Thorp, and Peter Mundy in *Infancy*, 2004, Vol. 6, No. 3, pages 397–406 and Messinger, Daniel. S. 2005. "A Measure of Early Joy? Afterword to the Re-publication of 'All Smiles Are Positive, but Some Smiles Are More Positive Than Others.'" Pp. 350–53 in *What the Face Reveals: Studies of Spontaneous Facial Expression Using the Facial Action Coding System (FACS)* 2d ed., edited by P. Ekman, P. and E. Rosenberg. Oxford University Press.

2. Davis 1947.

3. Cooley 1902.

4. Mead 1913.

5. National Association of Secretaries of State "New Millennium Project: American Youth Attitudes on Politics, Citizenship, Government, and Voting."

6. Web site for Camp Manitou.

7. Korgen 1999 p. 73.

8. The Pew Research Center 2002.

9. McAdam 1988.

❖ REFERENCES

Camp Manitou Web site. Accessed at http://www.manitoucamp.com/camp communication.htm on September 18, 2005

Cooley, Charles Horton. 1902. *Human Nature and the Social Order*. New York: Schocken Books.

Davis, Kingsley. 1947. "Final Note on a Case of Extreme Isolation." *American Journal of Sociology* 52 (5), March: 432–37.

Korgen, Odell Kathleen. 1999. *From Black to Biracial: Transforming Racial Identity Among Americans*. Westport: Praeger. P. 73.

McAdam, Doug. 1988. *Freedom Summer*. New York: Oxford University Press.

Mead, George Herbert. 1913. "The Social Self." *Journal of Philosophy, Psychology, and Scientific Methods* 10: 374–80.

Messinger, Daniel. 2005. "A Measure of Early Joy? Afterword to the Re-publication of 'All Smiles Are Positive, But Some Smiles Are More Positive Than Others.'" Pp. 350–53 in Paul Edman & Ericka Rosenberg (Eds.), *What the Face Reveals: Studies of Spontaneous Facial Expression Using the Facial Action Coding System (FACS)* 2d ed. New York: Oxford University Press.

National Association of Secretaries of State. 2000. "New Millennium Project: American Youth Attitudes on Politics, Citizenship, Government, and Voting." Accessed at http://www.nass.org/electioninfo/New%20Mil% 20Exec%20Summary.htm on September 9, 2005.

Ostrander, Susan. 2004. "Democracy, Civic Participation, and the University: A Comparative Study of Civic Engagement on Five Campuses." *Nonprofit and Voluntary Sector Quarterly* 33(1), March: 74–93.

The Pew Research Center. 2002. "Among Wealthy Nations . . . U.S. Stands Alone in Its Embrace of Religion." Accessed at http://people-press .org/reports/display.php3?ReportID=167 on May 23, 2006.

Venezia, Meaghan, Daniel S. Messinger, Danielle Thorp, and Peter Mundy. 2004. "The Development of Anticipatory Smiling." *Infancy*, 6(3): 397–406.

6

Social Institutions

Family and Economy

W hat do social institutions have to do with your life? A lot! The makeup of your family, the laws you must follow, your professional career, your schooling, and even whether or not you believe in a higher power (and, if so, what kind of higher power) are all based on the social institutions in your society. You begin your life among family, and learn about the world through educational institutions (schools), religious institutions (including rituals surrounding birth, marriage, and death), and cultural institutions (TV, anyone?). Much of your education is about preparing for life within structured economic institutions (jobs, the labor market).[1] All the while, your public life, and even your private one, is moved and shaped by the workings of political institutions. If the institutions change, so do you. Imagine how different your life would be if the United States did not uphold just one element of the bill of rights: the freedom, based in the first amendment, from unreasonable[2] monitoring of personal phone and email conversations.

How do we know an institution when we see one? In everyday language, physical places, like a jail, are sometimes referred to as institutions. But in sociology, "institutions" refer to a realm of public action with its own sets of organized rules and beliefs that direct how a society will carry out its basic needs. How do we know what is a basic need for a society? Create your own imaginary society and think about what you need to do for your society to survive. Keep in mind that you can eat what you like at home, but we all share the problem of where the garbage will go when you are done.

Imagine you and your fellow students are stranded on a distant planet that looks and feels like Earth but has no other human inhabitants. What is the first thing you would do? Almost certainly, you would (a) figure out what you need to do to survive and (b) start assigning people to those tasks you determined need doing. The first thing you would probably need to do is ensure some semblance of order for these undertakings. So, the first institution you would set up is some sort of *government*. (We're assuming that there are a lot of other students with you, not just a few classmates.) Secondly, you would have to start producing some food, finding water, and arranging for some system to distribute these goods. Whether you all share equally or distribute the goods according to some complex system of entitlements, you would be creating a system that includes ownership and "exchange value." In other words, you would be creating an *economic* institution, an institution that organizes how a society generates, allocates, and uses wares and services. Because the needs of your group on this distant world would be different from the needs of the society in which you actually live, you would not need the same institutions in the same way. But here is the interesting part about ideas and practices that become *institutionalized*: It is hard to imagine them differently. For that reason, you would have a very hard time creating a government or an economy that did not strongly resemble the one you know now (or at least one that you have read or heard about).

Although not everyone believes in or practices a religion, every known society has had some form of religious institution (just ask an Anthropologist). Would you and your companions adopt a unified system of belief to help you make sense of your new situation? If you were not rescued quickly, you might start (if you hadn't already!) trying to establish, in an organized way, a connection between yourselves and a higher power. Organizing a new or reestablishing an old religion (from Earth) might help you come to terms with your situation, feel that someone (or thing) was watching over you, and enable you to believe that, eventually (if only when you die) you would be going to a better place, seeing old loved ones, and so forth. If you remained on the island-world for more than a very short period of time, you would also have to set up rules about who could have sex with whom (to avoid nasty fights and to protect physically vulnerable members of the population) and (eventually) who should take care of the offspring of such unions (and how). In doing so, you would be establishing the institution of the *family*.

Finally, if you remained stuck on that planet, you would have to ensure that new members born into your society could learn your culture and the skills necessary to help your society survive. You would have to establish a social institution responsible for educating the members of your society. Once you had done so you would have established the fifth basic institution found in almost every society, an *educational system*.

As you have probably already noticed, these institutions are all related to one another. A functionalist would maintain that they are also all *interdependent*. Just as a living organism starts to die if a single one of its major organs (like the heart) starts to fail, functionalists maintain that if one institution is not working properly in a society, all the other ones (and the aggregate society) will suffer as well. For example, if our education system is not carrying out its function properly, young adults will not be prepared to get good jobs, and therefore will not be able to support a family, pay taxes, financially support their religious organizations, or buy goods. Eventually the faulty educational system would harm the family, economic, religious, and political institutions.

Unlike functionalists, conflict theorists examine the manner in which different interests in society work against one another. Karl Marx, for example, famously demonstrated that the worker class and the capitalist class were necessarily in conflict over just about everything that went on in society, from the organization of work to the proper use of police and courts to the workings of a free press. But conflict also occurs between social institutions.

Marx maintained that there was one institution that influenced and largely directed all the other institutions. According to Marx, as the type of economic system changed, so did the makeup of the other institutions. The government, the schools, the family, and religion were all tools for those who owned the means of production. Marxism, therefore, begins with the assumptions of *economic determinism*: that is, that the economic institutions shape the rest. Some political theorists, like Niccolo Machiavelli, are *political determinists*. (Machiavelli, who is most remembered for his classic text, *The Prince*, defined war as an extension of politics, merely another means by which leaders seek to extend their influence.) There are also those for whom religious institutions, or even social institutions (like systems of racial privilege) form the determining institution, with the rest following. Although all the major institutions are tied to one another in some way, in this chapter we will focus on the social institutions of the family and the economy.

Exercise 6.1 | **Functions of the Economy**

1. Imagine you live in a society in which the economic institution is not working properly (e.g., there is high unemployment or high inflation). According to the functionalist theoretical perspective, how might the decline in the economic institution affect the other institutions in society? Specifically, how would it affect the (a) family, (b) education, (c) religious, and (d) governmental institutions?

2. Now, imagine that you live in a society in which the economic institution is strong and thriving. According to the functionalist theoretical perspective, how might the thriving economic institution affect the other institutions in society? Specifically, how would it affect the (a) family, (b) education, (c) religious, and (d) governmental institutions?

❖ THE FAMILY

Marx maintained that relations between family members and even the average size of families are influenced by changes in the economic system. For example, under an agrarian economic system, in which work was centered on the family, families were large so that they would produce many workers to till the land and produce crops. When societies became industrialized and work shifted into factories and other centralized locations, families became smaller. The move from farm to city meant that families could no longer feed themselves through producing more food in the fields. More children meant more mouths had to be fed through low-wage work in factories.

According to Karl Marx's writing partner, Friedrich Engels, families maintain the economic system of capitalism and the existing class structure. Legal marriages were created so that men would be able to know clearly who their heirs were so that they could bequeath their wealth to their male offspring. A marriage contract transferred a kind of ownership of the bride from her father, whose name she bore, to the husband, whose name she adopted. The traditional patriarchal family structure also worked to perpetuate the capitalist economic system because it allowed men to devote themselves to making money while the wives took care of them, their children, and their home (for no pay). This system also contributed to the maintenance of gender inequality.

Whereas conflict theorists use a macro-level approach to see connections between families and economic systems, symbolic interactionists use a micro-level analysis to focus on how institutions influence the roles men and women play and the status they assume in the family. Even today, and even in the most egalitarian nations in the world, gender socialization within families contributes to inequality between men and women.

A sociological study that examined power dynamics among two-income couples in Sweden indicates socialization can trump earning power even in one of the most gender egalitarian societies in the world. Gender-based socialization is prevalent even in Sweden. Growing up, Swedish girls are more likely than Swedish boys to be taught that they should think of others before themselves. This gender-based socialization resulted in the fact that the women in the study tended to feel more responsible for taking care of such household needs as buying food and clothes for the children. They often used their own money to buy goods for the household. Even though they each had the same amount of money to spend, the women ended up having less money to use for themselves and, therefore, less power to determine how the couple's joint income should be spent. As the authors described the situation,

> the women in the study seemed to subordinate their own needs to those of other family members, yet did not see their behaviour as sacrifice. Instead, it seemed to be something that they did without reflecting over the reasons or consequences.

Therefore, even though both husbands and wives in Sweden are likely to say they should share their income equally, the "women seemed to experience less influence over economic decision making and less access to personal spending money."[3]

However, even though gender inequality remains, the institution of the family is changing. Across the globe, the marriage rate is falling and the cohabitation rate is rising. For example, whereas the divorce rate in the United States remains relatively consistent (at almost 50%), the percentage of babies born to unwed parents has increased steadily since the late 1990s. According to the Center for Disease Control's "National Vital Statistics Report 2003,"[4] 34.6% of all babies in the United States are now born to unmarried women. As Stephanie Coontz, the author of *Marriage, a History: From Obedience to Intimacy, or How Love Conquered Marriage*, states, "From Turkey to South Africa to Brazil, countries are having to codify the legal rights and obligations of single individuals and unmarried couples raising children, including same-sex couples."[5] The pattern is clear: Fewer children are being raised by married parents.

Other changes to the institution of the family are now taking place. For example, same-sex marriage is now legal in Massachusetts. Also, most mothers now work outside the home (as well as in it). Today,

72% of mothers between the ages of 15 and 44 work outside the home. The percentage of mothers with infants who are employed has also increased dramatically over the past 20 years (31% in 1976 to 55% today).[6] It's important to note that this is not a new phenomenon for women in poverty, particularly women of color.[7]

Exercise 6.2   The Changing American Family

There are multiple causes for the changes in the institution of the family noted above, both structural and cultural. However, there is ongoing debate as to whether these changes are more positive or negative for society. Write a 1-2 page essay that examines these changes in the family from either (a) a conflict perspective or (b) a functionalist perspective (If need be, refer to the descriptions of these perspectives in Chapter Two.) When writing your essay, be sure to

1. Provide an overview of how society operates according to that theoretical perspective and then apply that perspective to the changes in the social institution of the family.

2. Discuss whether or not someone coming from the theoretical perspective you chose would approve or disapprove of the changes in the family (and why or why not).

❖ THE ECONOMIC SYSTEM

Economies organize how a society creates, distributes, and uses its goods and services. Today, we live in a global economy in which the economic system of capitalism dominates. Goods and services are created and sold, for profit, across national borders at an increasingly rapid pace. Inequality among nations is related to what each contributes to and takes from the global economy. "Global north" nations (most postindustrial nations like the United States, Western European nations, and Japan) primarily contribute service work in the knowledge economy, with high skilled workers,[8] whereas "global south" nations (e.g., most Latin American, African, Middle Eastern, and Asian nations) tend to produce raw materials and/or provide cheap labor to produce goods consumed in global north nations. To participate in the knowledge economy, nations need strong educational, banking, and legal systems, like those found in global north countries. The nations with those assets have benefited the most from the globalization process while using their economic advantage to increase their power in determining global governance and the future of the global economy.

Other sectors of the world have not benefited as much from globalization. The World Trade Organization (WTO), which oversees the terms of global trade; the International Monetary Fund (IMF), which manages global financial markets; and the World Bank, which provides loans for economic development, are primarily controlled by global north nations and influenced by the concerns of global corporations. For the most part, these organizations have had a net effect of increasing the power and wealth of global north nations while decreasing the power, wealth, and quality of life in global south nations. For instance, between 1984 and 1990, IMF and World Bank loans resulted in the net transfer of wealth and resources from global south nations to global north nations of more than $150 billion.[9] For the most part, already poor nations have become even poorer as a result of the new global economy and the rules that give advantage to the already affluent nations. African, Latin American, and most Asian nations have very little bargaining power in the global economy and must find ways to compete in an economic system largely controlled by global north corporations and institutions.

For example, the United Nations' 2005 "Report on the World Social Situation: The Inequality Predicament" notes that

> the cumulative result of [global-north-encouraged] structural reform in Latin America over the past two decades has been a rise in inequality. . . . [Moreover], protectionist practices and agricultural subsidies in developed countries have led to a drop in agricultural productivity and, in turn, agricultural income. At present, the Latin American and Caribbean region imposes an 8.5 percent duty on non-agricultural imports from industrialized countries, but its own agricultural imports are subject to a 20.4 percent duty in industrialized countries, perpetuating rural poverty.[10]

Exercise 6.3   The World Trade Organization

1. Go to the WTO History Project at http://depts.washington.edu/wto hist/index.htm

2. Under "Resources" click on "top 10 documents."

3. Read at least two of each of the "Documents Not Produced by the WTO" and the "Documents Produced by the WTO."

— *(Continued)* —

—— (Continued) ——

4. Write a paper that answers either questions *a, b,* and *c* OR questions *d* and e:

   a. What groups or organizations are represented in each?

   b. As a sociologist, which documents do you think are most convincing? Explain why.

   c. Did you know very much about the WTO before reading this chapter and these documents? If yes, why? What gave you that knowledge? If not, why do you think you didn't know much about the WTO?

   d. How would a conflict theorist describe the function of the WTO?

   e. How would a functionalist theorist describe the function of the WTO?

Exercise 6.4   **Critiquing Modern Globalization**

1. Go to the Global Exchange Web page and read the following Fact Sheets: http://www.globalexchange.org/campaigns/wbimf/facts.html and http://www.globalexchange.org/campaigns/sweatshops/sweatshopsfaq.html.pf.

2. Write a 1–2 page essay outlining the major arguments being presented against the current manner of globalization.

Exercise 6.5   **From Free Trade to Fair Trade**

1. Read "10 Ways to Democratize the Global Economy" at http://www.globalexchange.org/campaigns/wbimf/TenWaysToDemocratize.html.pf.

2. Write an essay outlining the suggestions made by the authors to move toward a different form of globalization. Do you agree or disagree with the authors? Think of some suggestions you might add and outline how they might be carried out.

Growing levels of inequality can also be seen *within* global north nations. In the United States, inequalities have steadily increased over the past 20 years, despite consistent growth in most measures of national economic health. In most states, middle-income families have seen a drop in their incomes during the 1990s, adjusting for inflation, whereas incomes increased substantially among the wealthiest 20%.[11] Whereas the richest 1% of Americans possessed 20% of the wealth in 1975, by 2001, the richest 1% of Americans owned a full one-third (33%) of the wealth of all Americans.[12] A June 2005 article in *The New York Times* entitled "Richest Are Leaving Even the Rich Far Behind" pointed out that, in recent years, the richest Americans "have pulled far ahead of the rest of the population, . . . [and] have even left behind people making hundreds of thousands of dollars a year."[13] Even more startling is the fact that the poorest 20% of people (more than 50 million Americans) have actually become poorer since 1980.[14] One of the most drastic outcomes of these trends in wealth and poverty is that there are currently nearly 40 million Americans living in or at-risk of hunger.[15]

Many of the hungry are the working poor. The following quote from "Betsy," a middle-aged mother in *Hungry to Be Heard: Voices From a Malnourished America*[16] illustrates this fact:

> Right now I'm holding down two different jobs, one that's pretty much full-time and then another one that gives me about 20 hours or so a week and this is six days a week that I'm working now. And I work hard, too, . . . I work real hard, and I'm tired from it as well. . . . But no matter [how hard I work] when it gets time to pay the bills we simply can't get by on what I'm making. . . . Minimum wage at one place and a little better at the other doesn't help me enough in terms of feeding my children, paying the bills, and providing as I need to for them.

At the low end of the global economic spectrum, men, women, and children find themselves forced to try to make a living on farms that can not compete with global agribusinesses (as seen above) or through minimum wage jobs or labor in "sweatshop" factories that offer low wages, hard work, and no benefits. As the quote above illustrates, the result is often hunger and deprivation for the workers and their families.

Although sweatshops are most common in global south nations because of lack of unions and inadequately enforced (if they exist at all) labor laws in such nations, there also remain pockets of sweatshops in global north nations as well, including many right here in the United States. Recognizing the existence of sweatshops in their own city and throughout the globe, the city government of San Francisco recently declared a campaign against sweatshops worldwide. The *San Francisco Chronicle* described the campaign and the problem of sweatshops this way:

By launching a campaign to eliminate worldwide sweatshop-labor abuse, San Francisco Mayor Gavin Newsom and Supervisor Tom Ammiano made a powerful statement denouncing a global travesty. From China to Mexico, garment workers—many of whom are young children—work up to 15 hours a day with no bathroom or eating breaks and make as little as 13 cents an hour.

But tucked away in San Francisco's South of Market and in pockets of the Mission District, those who are looking can find similar conditions right here at home. These workers are mostly middle-age and older immigrant women, who have little education and speak no English. They work up to 12 hours a day with few or no breaks and get paid by "piece rates," meaning, per garment. On average, this adds up to $1 or $2 an hour.[17]

The city of San Francisco is far from alone in its campaign against sweatshops. According to Global Exchange,[18]

in 2003, California passed legislation that sets no-sweat standards for the procurement of state clothing such as uniforms. Three other states—Maine, New Jersey, and Pennsylvania—have similar laws in place. Twenty-six cities, 28 school districts, and 10 counties also have no-sweat procurement regulations.[19]

College students have been some of the most powerful opponents of sweatshops. On campuses across the nation, undergraduates have been striving to make sure that the apparel sold on their campus is made in sweat-free factories. More than 40 universities (such as Boston College, Michigan State University, Yale, University of Southern Mississippi, and UC Irvine), have joined the United Students Against Sweatshops' (USAS) "Sweat Free" Campus Campaign.[20]

Exercise 6.6	Students Creating Change: The Anti-Sweatshop Movement

Go to the USAS Web site at http://www.studentsagainstsweatshops.org/.

Write a two-page paper that describes (a) one campaign on which the USAS is currently working, (b) whether or not you could see yourself joining that campaign, and (c) why you could or could not see yourself participating in the campaign.

Exercise 6.7   **Work, Unemployment, and Our Changing Economy**

Go to the Web site for the U.S. Department of Labor Bureau of Labor Statistics at http://www.bls.gov/oes/home.htm and search for "Mass Layoffs Summary." Read the most recent Mass Layoffs Summary and answer the following questions:

1. What were the top three reasons (in order) for the most recent mass layoffs?

2. Which metropolitan area was most affected by recent mass layoffs?

3. How does the most recent quarterly report on mass layoffs compare to those of the previous 4 years?

Now go to http://www.google.com. Search for "Unemployment Insurance and [name of your state]."

1. What percentage of their salary would the unemployed receive in unemployment insurance (assuming they met the eligibility requirements for maximum unemployment insurance coverage in your state)?

2. For how long could they collect unemployment insurance?

3. How well do you think they could support themselves or a family on unemployment insurance? Elaborate.

Exercise 6.8   **Immigration and Citizenship**

Imagine you have a friend in Mexico who would like to come to the United States to make more money to support his or her family. You want to try to help him or her.

1. Go to the U.S. Citizenship and Immigration homepage at http://uscis.gov/graphics/index.htm.

2. After looking at this Web site, how would you guide your Mexican friend in his or her effort to come to the United States?

3. What would make acquiring a green card fairly simple?

4. Do you think most Mexicans who would like to immigrate to the United States are able to do so legally, if they choose to do so? Why or why not?

Sociologist in Action: Alan Ashbaugh

In the following paragraphs, recent college graduate Alan Ashbaugh describes how he uses the sociological tools he gained as a sociology major at Colby College in Maine to bring about social justice locally, nationally, and globally.

Studying sociology greatly influenced the course of my life, giving me the tools to examine the social world, the skills and inspiration to affect positive change, and the direction to use my sociological training meaningfully and effectively.

In my sociology classes at Colby College, Waterville, Maine, I learned about the nature of society, the harsh and complex realities of social issues, and, most importantly, that change toward a more just world is possible. A sociological truth that I will always remember is that society is not a static, unstoppable force, as it is so often referred to in popular media, but it is instead a constantly emerging and shifting combination of individuals making decisions and taking action. Thus, the world is already changing; we need only to guide it in the right direction by taking effective social action.

Of the many issues we explored in my introductory sociology course, the one that stood out for me is the vast economic inequality in my own community and internationally, as well as the social classes that create and perpetuate these inequalities. A subsequent sociology course on globalization broadened my sociological perspective to focus on the global issues of poverty, inequality, and justice, and the impact of each individual's actions on people worldwide. Examining these issues led me to a more vivid understanding of the social world, issues in my local and international communities, and a better sense of my place in Colby, Waterville, and society as a whole. This newfound understanding inspired me to get involved on and off campus, using my sociological training to move toward change. I became a founding leader of the Colby South End Coalition, which addresses the social and economic divide between Colby and its hometown of Waterville by encouraging volunteerism, dialogue, and a coming together of the two communities. I also took on the role as head of Colby Habitat for Humanity, which tackled economic inequality locally by connecting low-income families with decent, affordable housing. Moving beyond Waterville in scope, for the 2004 presidential election I helped to organize the Voter Coalition to "get out the vote," and I traveled to Chile to investigate the social promise of the emerging concept of Corporate Social Responsibility.

Graduating from Colby in May 2005, I did not have a set career path. I only knew that I loved raising awareness of social issues and bringing students together to take action, and that I wanted to continue to be socially active beyond college. My senior year I had the good fortune of learning about a job opportunity at an organization called Free the Children through an inspiring, socially involved professor in the Sociology department. Free the Children was founded in 1995 by a 12-year-old boy named Craig Kielburger, who was so appalled at the practice of child labor he had read about in the newspaper that he gathered a group of his friends and classmates to raise awareness and take action to effect change—exactly what I was passionate about. In the past 10 years, Free the Children has grown to become the largest network of children helping children through education, having built over 400 schools, educating more than 35,000 children every day, sent more than $9 million worth of medical supplies, and implemented alternative income projects benefiting more than 20,000 people in developing countries. Free the Children's mission and the work they do matched my own personal goals and beliefs, so I applied for the position just prior to graduation and was hired!

Today, as an International Youth Coordinator at Free the Children, I provide youth with the tools to make a difference in the world, such as information on social issues, effective fundraising and awareness-raising techniques, and the public speaking skills to powerfully communicate their passion to their peers. I use my sociological training each day in my work at Free the Children in examining the social issues that we are working to change, discovering the best ways to encourage and enable young people to effect positive change, and beyond. The image of society I formed from my sociology classes of a constantly emerging collection of individual actions, in conjunction with the social issues we studied, help me to remember every day the power that each individual has to make a huge difference and the tremendous importance of doing so.

SOURCE: Courtesy of Alan Ashbaugh.

❖ DISCUSSION QUESTIONS

1. What role do you think economic globalization plays in legal and illegal immigration to the United States?

2. How do you think families support (or do not support) the current economic system in the United States?

3. How has your socialization process affected the roles you play in your family?

4. How has your socialization process affected the roles you play in the U.S. economy?

5. If you marry, do you think you will share domestic chores equally with your spouse? Why or why not?

6. Imagine that the institution of the family suddenly disappeared. How might our society be different without this primary institution? Do you think our society could survive without it? Why or why not?

❖ SUGGESTIONS FOR SPECIFIC ACTIONS

1. Research the family-related personnel policies at your college. Do you think they provide adequate benefits for employees who must care for a sick family member? If not, come up with a reasonable suggestion for policy reform and work with your student government leaders to present your ideas (and advocate for them) to the administration.

2. Research the policies that your college has for providing benefits to partners of LGBTI (Lesbian, Gay, Bisexual, Transgender, Intersexed) employees. Are they the same as for the partners of heterosexual employees? If not, why not? How do your findings, in either case, reflect the values of your college (*your* institution!) and of the greater society? If you find inequalities and believe they need to be changed, what steps could you take to ensure that the partners of all employees receive equal benefits?[21]

3a. Go to the Immigration and Customs Enforcement Students and Exchange Visitors Web page at http://www.ice.gov/sevis/index.htm

3b. Interview the administrator on your campus who is in charge of International Students. Ask him or her how your school assists international students through the process of becoming visiting students on your campus.

3c. Interview five international students at your school. Ask them about the steps they went through to become visiting students at your school. Be sure to note any differences in their experiences and why these differences may have occurred (the year of their matriculation, the nation from which they came, their economic status, etc.).

3d. Use this information to create a resource for international students that could be put on your school Web site (if approved by your college or university administration).

4. Go to www.freethechildren.com After browsing through the Web site, go to the section that provides information on Child Labor and read this information (http://www.freethechildren.com/getinvolved/geteducated/childlabour.htm). One of the most powerful ways to fight against child labor is to ensure that children have schools to attend and the resources (school fees, books, uniforms, etc.) to afford to go. Now that you know about child labor and how important education is, you can start a campaign to raise money to build schools in child labor heavy regions. Check out the resources at http://www.freethechildren.com/getinvolved/buildaschool.htm and begin a school-building campaign at your college.

Please go to our Web site at http://www.sagepub.com/korgen to find further civic engagement opportunities, resources, and peer-reviewed articles related to this chapter.

❖ ENDNOTES

1. Of course, some leave high school and join the military institution. Many do this in hopes of receiving the training and experience they need to succeed economically once they leave the military.

2. As this book was being written, Americans were debating the extent of the first-amendment–based freedom from unreasonable monitoring of personal phone and e-mail conversations.

3. Nyman 1999, p. 789.

4. Center for Disease Control 2003.

5. Coontz 2005.

6. U.S. Census Bureau 2005.

7. Coontz 1992.

8. Garrett 2004.

9. Sports for Hunger, "Fact Sheet: World Bank and IMF" 2004. Accessed at www.sportsforhunger.org on December 28, 2005.

10. To see the full report, go to http://www.un.org/esa/socdev/rwss/media%2005/cd-docs/media.htm.

11. Larin and McNichol 1997.

12. Beeghley 2005.

13. Johnston 2005.

14. Shapiro et al. 2001.

15. The Food Research and Action Center (FRAC) 2005.

16. White.

17. From "Sweatshop Crackdown," June 30, in *San Francisco Chronicle.* Copyright © 2005, San Francisco Chronicle. Reprinted with permission.

18. See http://www.globalexchange.org/campaigns/sweatshops/back ground.html.

19. For example, the city of Bangor, Maine passed legislation stating: "All clothes available on local store shelves should be made according to established international standards of ethical production." See http://www.pica .ws/cc/bgrccc.htm.

20. For more information about the campaign, go to http://www .studentsagainstsweatshops.org/campaigns/sweatfree_dday.php.

21. It is also important to note that being offered policies such as health insurance does not change the inequality in taxation that results from lack of recognition of the partner by the federal government. For example, if the partner from a same sex couple uses $20,000 worth of benefits, the partner with the medical benefits is taxed as if she earned that $20,000. So, equal benefits are a start but not a solution to this issue of inequality.

❖ REFERENCES

Beeghley, Leonard. 2005. *The Structure of Social Stratification in the United States.* Boston: Pearson.

Center for Disease Control. 2003. *National Vital Statistics Report 2003,* Volume 54, No 2. Accessed at http://www.cdc.gov/nchs/data/nvsr/nvsr54/ nvsr54_02.pdf on October 7, 2005.

Coontz, Stephanie. 1992. *The Way We Never Were: American Families and the Nostalgia Trap.* New York: Basic Books.

Coontz, Stephanie. 2005. "For Better, For Worse: Marriage Means Something Different Now." *Washingtonpost.com,* May 1. Accessed at http://www .washingtonpost.com/wp-dyn/content/article/2005/04/30/AR200504 3000108_pf.html on January 2, 2006.

The Food Research and Action Center (FRAC). 2005. "Hunger in the US." Accessed at http://www.frac.org/html/hunger_in_the_us/hunger_index .html on November 28, 2005.

Garrett, Geoffrey. 2004. *Trade Blocs and Social Integration.* Presented at the Trade Blocs, Neoliberalism, and the Quality of Life in Latin America Conference, UCLA Latin American Center, June. Accessed at http://www.isop.ucla .edu/lac/article.asp?parentid=12060 on June 10, 2005.

Johnston, David Cay. 2005. "Richest Are Leaving Even the Rich Far Behind." *New York Times,* June 5, p. A1.

Larin, Kathryn and Elizabeth McNichol. 1997. "Pulling Apart: A State by State Analysis of Income Trends." Center on Budget and Policy Priorities. Accessed at http://www.cbpp.org/pa-1.htm on November 20, 2005.

Machiavelli, Niccolo. *The Prince*, translated by N.H. Thomson. Vol. XXXVI, Part 1. The Harvard Classics. New York: P.F. Collier & Son, 1909–14; Bartleby.com, 2001. Accessed at http://www.bartleby.com/36/1/ on May 24, 2006.

Nyman, Charlott. 1999. "Gender equality in 'the most equal country in the world'? Money and marriage in Sweden." *Sociological Review*, 47(4), November 1: 766–793.

San Francisco Chronicle. 2005. "Sweatshop Crackdown." June 30, p. B8. Accessed at http://www.sfgate.com/cgi-bin/article.cgi?file=/chronicle/archive/2005/06/30/EDGOODGAUA1.DTL on November 28, 2005.

Shapiro, Isaac, Robert Greenstein, and Wendell Primus. 2001. "Pathbreaking CBO Study Shows Dramatic Increases in Income Disparities in 1980s and 1990s: An Analysis of the CBO Data." Accessed at Center on Budget and Policy Priorities Web site, http://www.cbpp.org/5-31-01tax.htm on November 28, 2005.

U.S. Census Bureau. 2005. "Facts for Features." Accessed at http://www.census.gov/Press-Release/www/releases/archives/facts_ for_features_ special_editions/004109.html on October 7, 2005.

White, Jonathan M. Forthcoming. *Hungry to be Heard: Voices From a Malnourished America*. Oxford: Oxford University Press.

7

Social Institutions, Continued

Education, Government, and Religion

S hould students in U.S. public schools be required to pledge allegiance to the flag of the United States of America and to the Republic for which it stands, one nation under God, indivisible, with liberty and justice for all? This question reveals the connection between educational, political, and religious institutions in the United States. How is God connected to our nation? What God? Whose God? Are you less of an American if you don't believe in a God? And why is this question yielding a political fight now?[1] These queries have been debated by politicians, religious leaders, and educators across the United States. In this chapter, we examine the institutions of education, government, and religion and their relationship to one another and the other primary institutions in U.S. society.

❖ EDUCATIONAL INSTITUTIONS

As noted in Chapter Six, educational institutions teach young members of society the basic and (in some cases) advanced skills needed to function effectively in our society. In turn, educated citizens enable societies to run smoothly and to become more technologically advanced, more productive, and more prosperous. The educational level of a nation's population is directly related to its level of income inequality and overall economic health.[2]

As other key institutions in society change, so do the functions of the educational system. For example, as economies change, so do the skills needed and taught in the educational systems. You are undoubtedly aware of the fact that nowadays most new jobs that pay well require at least a college education. This is very different from a half century ago, when it was possible (at least for White men) to earn a good salary by working in a factory with a strong union. No college degree was required or expected for such positions and only a small percentage of the population completed college.

In the United States, educational institutions are also connected in a variety of ways to the institution of government. State and local governments provide most of the funding for public schools. In most states, primary and secondary public schools receive funding based largely on local property taxes. Both the state and federal government create educational goals. In recent years, the federal government has played a larger role in regulating the function and operation of public schools, even though the federal government provides only about 8% of funding for public schools. For example, the federally mandated No Child Left Behind Act has established test-focused goals and timetables that public schools must adhere to in order to receive federal funding.

Most of what occurs within our schools is determined or administered by local governments. School boards, whose members consist of locally elected or appointed members, oversee the operation of schools and create goals at the local level that are consistent with state and federal laws. Although they do have greater freedom in determining curriculum, even private schools are bound to abide by U.S. laws, such as antidiscrimination laws. In short, government fingerprints can be found at all levels of the institution of education, in school curricula, school buildings, and pedagogical approaches.

All three of the institutions examined in this chapter are evident when we look at the 2002 No Child Left Behind Act[3] and the school boards that are working to put this legislation into action. Through this law, the federal government allows religious organizations to receive federal education grants to run after-school programs for students in the public education system. The merits of forming or sustaining other connections between religion and public schools are fought over, in many areas of the country, among local school board members and their supporters.

One of the most heated school board battles has centered on whether to teach intelligent design or evolution in science classes. Proponents of the faith-based idea of intelligent design, the notion that some intelligent, supernatural force was responsible for the creation of the world, have tried to influence the composition of school boards in their efforts to have this belief represented in the public school curriculum. Elected members of the State Board of Education in Kansas, for example, recently changed that state's science curriculum to include the Christian notion of "intelligent design" in science classes alongside of the teaching of evolution, whereas residents of Dover, Pennsylvania voted out all eight of their local school board members after the board had proposed to do the same thing there.[4] As of 2005, state and school officials in 16 states were debating the issue.[5]

Exercise 7.1	How Are Your Local Schools Funded?

Find the official Web page of your local school board by going to an Internet search engine (e.g., Google.com, Yahoo.com, etc.) and searching for the name of your town or city and the phrase "school board." Write a 1–2 page paper that answers the following questions:

1. How are your local schools funded?

2. Has funding increased or decreased over the past few years (and why)?

3. How do people become school board members? Are they elected? Are they appointed (and if so, by whom)?

4. What are the political affiliations of the members of your school board (e.g., How many Democrats? How many Republicans? Any independents or other party affiliations?)

5. How has the school addressed the federal No Child Left Behind Act? (This information should be on the school board Web site.)

6. Overall, according to the school board Web site, what are the key challenges facing your local public schools? How does the board claim to be addressing these challenges?

7. Now, imagine you are an official member of the school board. What two key challenges do you want to focus on? These may be similar to the ones that the board has identified or they may be your own, based on the research you have done. Outline these challenges and then describe several ideas you would suggest to address these challenges. For at least one of these suggestions for change, elaborate upon your plan and discuss in detail how your skills as a sociologist can help create this change.

❖ GOVERNMENT

The U.S. constitution sets the framework for governance in the United States. As anyone who has ever taken an American government or history course (or watched *Schoolhouse Rock)* knows, the Preamble to the Constitution describes what the founders of this nation hoped to gain from establishing their government under the Constitution.

> We, the people of the United States, in order to form a more perfect Union, establish justice, insure domestic tranquility, provide for the common defense, promote the general welfare, and secure the blessings of liberty to ourselves and our posterity, do ordain and establish this Constitution for the United States of America.

As the Preamble indicates, the government regulates a wide range of interactions and processes in our society. Government is responsible for the smooth functioning of society. This broad mandate includes ensuring public safety, from personal safety in neighborhoods to making sure that levees are properly built and maintained to protect citizens from flooding,[6] to overseeing public commerce (everything from an efficient transportation system to stable financial markets), to running fair and democratic elections. The government, in short, is responsible for overseeing the well-being and social welfare of the nation's citizens.

However, the majority of Americans do not actually exercise the power they have to elect their governmental representatives. Many do not even know who their elected representatives are, never mind whether or not they are actually "promot[ing] the general welfare." Only about half of all Americans who are eligible to vote exercise that right in presidential elections. Far fewer tend to vote in nonpresidential, local elections.

Many Americans feel disconnected from the political process and are turned off by the huge amounts of money spent on the campaigns they see covered on television. However, unlike national or statewide elections that involve millions of dollars and depend in great part upon who can raise the most money, local elections are more open to people who commit the resources of time and energy to cultivating local contacts and to urging people personally and in small groups to vote for them. Just as many state and national politicians spend much of their energy focused on potential larger donors, most local political hopefuls spend their energies trying to persuade community leaders to convince their own followers to vote for them. Therefore, although organized money is more important in state and federal elections, in local elections organized people can propel one to office. However, in all cases, those running for election or reelection to political posts can safely ignore people who do not stay involved in politics and who are not likely to vote.

Exercise 7.2   How Does Your Representative Vote?

1. Go to http://www.house.gov/

2. Look up your representative in the House of Representatives in Congress and find his or her Web page.

3. Find the last five votes cast by your representative.

4. Answer the following questions:

    a. Do you agree with the votes? (In other words, do they represent you?) Why or why not?

    b. Will you vote in the next election? Why or why not?

    c. Does reading about how your representative has voted recently make you more or less interested in voting for or against him or her in the next election? Why?

    d. If you do not agree with his or her vote on one or more issues, what actions can you (as a citizen) take to express your dissatisfaction?

    e. What actions can you take toward having your representative vote more to your liking on future issues?

❖ RELIGIOUS INSTITUTIONS

In 2001, 76.5% of Americans said they were Christian. The term "Christian" encompasses a plethora of religions ranging from mainstream Protestant to Evangelical Protestant to Catholic. Almost one out of four (24.5%) Americans are Catholic, making this the largest Christian group. Smaller religious groups include Muslim (.5%), Buddhist (.5%), and Jewish (1.3%). Slightly more than 14% of Americans did not affiliate themselves with a religious group (up from 8.2% in 1990).[7] Since 1990, Muslims and Buddhists have doubled in number (there are now more of each than there are Episcopalians), whereas the number of Jewish people in the United States has declined.[8,9]

Portrayals of religious institutions differ rather dramatically among the three primary theoretical perspectives in Sociology. These theories help us to understand the different roles religions play in society, how religions adapt to changes in society, and how they influence society and individuals in it. It is important to note that sociologists are interested in the interaction between religion and society rather than in the veracity of the teachings of a particular religion.

Following Durkheim's famous writings in this area, functionalists maintain that religion serves several functions for society. It unites its followers, helps establish order by providing a "correct" way of living, and gives people a sense of meaning and purpose in their lives. Of course, this particular functional analysis of religion assumes that there is only one religion in the society and does not consider societies with multiple religions, such as ours.

Conflict theorists argue that religions tend to distract oppressed people and prevent them from concentrating on the inequities of their societies. Marx once described religion as "the opium of the people."[10] He argued that religion helped maintain the status quo by encouraging workers to ignore their sufferings here on Earth, thus acting as an "opiate" by keeping the oppressed subdued and uninterested in rising up against their oppressors. The clergy, financially supported by the class of owners, counseled their followers not to protest the inequality that led to their poor conditions but rather to be docile and "good" here on Earth so that they could receive their reward for their earthly suffering and forbearance in Heaven.[11]

Symbolic interactionists point out that religions are socially constructed, created and recreated by followers through the use of symbols and rituals. They agree with functionalists that religion gives order to our lives. However, they also stress that individuals have agency and play active and consistent roles in the design and maintenance of their religion. Just as societies change and people create, adjust, and discard symbols, religious institutions change as well. For example, the change in symbols and attitudes within the Catholic Church brought about by the Second Vatican Council (1962–1965), changed the outlook of the church and many of its rules. The language of the mass changed from Latin to the tongue of the parishioners, the priest no longer faced away from his parishioners when saying mass, and guitars and folk groups replaced many organs and choirs. These symbolic shifts changed how members of the church related to one another and saw their roles within the church. Just changing certain symbols helped foster a rise in status of the Catholic laity and created a Catholic Church that Catholics who lived 100 years ago would scarcely recognize.

❖ THE RELATIONSHIPS AMONG EDUCATIONAL, GOVERNMENTAL, AND RELIGIOUS INSTITUTIONS

Like all other major institutions in society, educational, governmental, and religious institutions must find a way to coexist. Depending on your theoretical perspective, the grounds of this coexistence can vary widely (e.g., functionalists maintain that they can cooperate for the good of the whole society, whereas conflict theorists argue that the educational, governmental, religious, and family institutions merely carry out the desires of those who control the economic institution). However, no matter your theoretical perspective, it is clear that these institutions must interact with one another in a variety of ways.

For instance, just as we can find examples of the connection between educational and governmental institutions, there is also a clear interrelationship among the religious, educational, and governmental institutions. However, the influence of religion on government and educational systems varies widely from society to society. The laws of some societies are based on religious doctrines. In other societies, religions are not even officially acknowledged by the government.

❖ THE RELATIONSHIP AMONG RELIGION, GOVERNMENT, AND EDUCATION: COMPARING THE UNITED STATES AND FRANCE

Due in part to the fact that there was no one dominant religious organization at the time of the founding of the United States, the First Amendment to the U.S. Constitution contains the phrase "Congress shall make no law respecting an establishment of religion, or prohibiting the free exercise thereof." There is an inherent tension between the two clauses in this phrase. Some people stress the separation between church and state whereas others emphasize the Amendment's declaration that government cannot prohibit the exercise of religion.

Although there is no officially state-sponsored religion in the United States, there are obvious examples of the influence of religion on our government. From the words "In God We Trust" on our money to the routine inclusion of religious imagery in speeches by our Presidents, the imagery prevalent throughout the United States is Christian. France, on the other hand, has a constitution that does not even mention religious differences among its people. In France, people are free to practice whatever religion they would like, but they must do so in a private manner. In the United States, religious organizations are given tax-exempt status and recognized and honored by political leaders, but the French government's only official relationship with religious organizations is to make sure they do not infringe upon the liberty of others. Unlike in the United States, where some advocate bringing back compulsory prayer in schools and where there is an ongoing debate about requiring students to say a pledge that includes the word "God" in it, religion is specifically forbidden from public schools in France. In keeping with laws that prohibit public displays of religion, not only can students not pray publicly, they may not wear religious garb (such as head coverings) in school, even if their religion mandates that they wear such things in public.

Although U.S. law prohibits the government from endorsing or sanctioning one religion over another, it does not in any way prevent citizens from invoking religious grounds as a basis for their voting or other political participation, even to the point of forming national social movements to change the law. For example,

> In the 1830s, temperance and antislavery [movements] mobilized hundreds of thousands of Americans in a wave of confessional protests. In these protests, men and women gathered together to bear witness against what they deemed as the sins of drinking and slavery to pledge fellowship with reform societies, and to demand that religious and civil institutions repent. They were met with fierce resistance, and much of it was violent.[12]

Yet, in both of those cases, the goals of the movements were eventually adopted as law. What is significant here is that Christian activists, believing that drinking or slavery was morally wrong, led a movement to change the laws concerning drinking or slavery but not to change the laws concerning the role of religion in society.

In the United States, public schools are educational institutions, mandated by law, funded and regulated by government, and answerable to all citizens. Is it possible to have religious practices within a public school system without violating the laws mandating the separation of church and state? Consider the case described in Exercise 7.3.

Of course, not all those who say they are members of a religion actually attend religious services. According to Gallup International, 47% of North Americans attend church regularly (once a week or more) compared to 20% of Western Europeans and 14% of Eastern Europeans.[13] On the other hand, it is possible to believe in a God and feel connected to that God without attending religious services. According to the same

Exercise 7.3   School Sports and Prayer

The Bill of Rights Institute's Web site[14] lists the landmark Supreme Court cases that deal with the tension between the separation of church and state and freedom to worship clauses in the First Amendment. Santa Fe Independent School District v. Doe (2000) is one of the more recent decisions. For this case, Justice Stevens wrote the following for the majority opinion of the court (three Justices dissented).[15]

Prior to 1995, a student elected as Santa Fe High School's student council chaplain delivered a prayer over the public address system before each home varsity football game. Respondents, Mormon and Catholic students or alumni and their mothers, filed a suit challenging this practice and others under the Establishment Clause of the First Amendment. While the suit was pending, petitioner school district (District) adopted a different policy, which authorizes two student elections, the first to determine whether "invocations" should be delivered at games, and the second to select the spokesperson to deliver them. After the students held elections authorizing such prayers and selecting a spokesperson, the District Court entered an order modifying the policy to permit only nonsectarian, nonproselytizing prayer. The Fifth Circuit held that, even as modified by the District Court, the football prayer policy was invalid.

Held: The District's policy permitting student-led, student-initiated prayer at football games violates the Establishment Clause. Pp. 9–26.

(a) The Court's analysis is guided by the principles endorsed in *Lee v. Weisman,* 505 U.S. 577. There, in concluding that a prayer delivered by a rabbi at a graduation ceremony violated the Establishment Clause, the Court held that, at a minimum, the Constitution guarantees that government may not coerce anyone to support or participate in religion or its exercise, or otherwise act in a way that establishes a state religion or religious faith, or tends to do so, *id.,* at 587. The District argues unpersuasively that these principles are inapplicable because the policy's messages are private student speech, not public speech. The delivery of a message such as the invocation here—on school property, at school-sponsored events, over the school's public address system, by a speaker representing the student body, under the supervision of school faculty, and pursuant to a school policy that explicitly and implicitly encourages public prayer—is not properly characterized as "private" speech.

1. Do you agree with this opinion? Why or why not?

2. What might a symbolic interactionist say about the use of symbols by those carrying out these prayers? What do these symbols convey to the students and other fans attending the games? In particular, what do they imply about the appropriateness of public praying at football games?

3. What might a conflict theorist say about the court's decision?

poll, 83% of North Americans versus 49% of Eastern and Western Europeans rate God as having high importance in their lives.

Exercise 7.4	The Role of Religion in the Lives of Individuals

Survey 10 people about their religion. In the survey, include questions about (a) their religious membership (if they have one), (b) how often they go to religious services, and (c) if they think their belief in God guides their actions during an average day.

Then interview them, asking them to provide examples to illustrate their answers. Compare the results of your surveys and interviews. Were the findings consistent? Why or why not?

❖ THE 2005 RIOTS IN FRANCE

The riots in France in October and November of 2005 provide an example of how the relationships among educational, governmental, and religious institutions can go awry. Most of the rioters were poor teenagers of North African and Arab descent whose parents immigrated to France a generation ago when jobs were plentiful. The unemployment rate in the neighborhoods where people rioted hovers around 40% (compared to the rate of 10% throughout all of France). The rioters and their families also face discrimination in housing and in the French criminal justice system. Finishing or dropping out of school without skills needed to attain a job and facing racial–ethnic discrimination in the workforce, their employment prospects are dim.[16]

Today, those who participated in the 2005 riots in France face both racial and religious discrimination in a society that recognizes neither racial nor religious differences. Although it appears that most of those who rioted have *parents* who are practicing Muslims, the rioters did not riot because of religious beliefs. In fact, they are largely alienated from religious as well as governmental and educational institutions in France.[17] Whereas a Marxist might argue that they were able to rise up because they were not hindered by the "opium" of religion, a functionalist would point out that, as nonpracticing Muslims, they do not have the influence of religious organizations to help them establish a sense of purpose in their lives. Symbolic interactionists might also note that the rioters are not part of an organization (either religious or secular) constructed to effectively advocate for them and make sure that their demands are addressed by the French government.

Exercise 7.5   Governmental Response to the 2005 French Riots

Immediately after the 2005 riots, some French government leaders promised to reform the schooling system to better educate and prepare French youth for available jobs. Others questioned the government's practice of ignoring racial and religious differences among French citizens and advocated for the establishment of racial and religious statistical categories so that the government can discern patterns of racial and ethnic discrimination.

Use an Internet search engine to do a current search on information about the 2005 French riots. Use the terms "French" and "riot," "2005," "policy," and "reform" to conduct your search. Write a two-page paper that briefly describes the riots and two to three reforms the French government enacted in response to them. Then list two or three reforms that you think still need to be enacted. Choose one of these and write a one-page paper describing the details of how the government can make and monitor this change.

Sociologists in Action: David Brunsma and Kerry Rocquemore

Are school uniforms an easy fix for problems in U.S. public schools? Many people have proposed that uniforms would reduce status competition among school kids, including violent competition. Proponents of school uniforms maintain that they help to create a sense of belonging and communal feeling among students while also fostering a greater sense of discipline. Although this hypothesis appears reasonable, there was no actual data until sociologists David Brunsma and Kerry Rocquemore conducted a sociological study to determine the effects of school uniforms on substance abuse, behavioral problems, attendance, and academic achievement among 10th graders.[18] Using data from a 1994 follow-up study on the National Educational Longitudinal Study of 1988, Brunsma and Rocquemore revealed that school uniforms had no direct effect on substance abuse, behavioral problems, or attendance and a slight *negative* effect on academic achievement. When improvements were seen, they were related to other factors (funded attempts to change course content, improve pedagogy, etc.).

(Continued)

(Continued)

In the words of Brunsma and Rocquemore,

> Instituting a uniform policy can be viewed as analogous to cleaning and brightly painting a deteriorating building in that on the one hand it grabs our immediate attention; on the other hand, it is only a coat of paint. That type of change attracts attention to schools and implies the presence of serious problems that necessitate drastic change. It seems possible that such attention renews an interest on the parts of parents and communities and provides possibilities for supporting additional types of organizational change. . . .
>
> [However], the nature and magnitude of the support behind the mandatory uniform policies . . . seem to illustrate the quick fix nature of school reform policies in the 1990s. A policy that is simplistic, readily understandable, cost free (to taxpayers), and appealing to common sense is one that is politically pleasing and, hence, finds much support. When challenged with broader reforms, those policies with results not immediately identifiable and those that are costly and demand energy and a willingness to change on the part of school faculty and parents are unacceptable.

Through this research, Brunsma and Rocquemore shed light on arguments and strategies for school reform that had theretofore been driven by political agendas (pressure for quick fixes without spending money) and anecdotal and incomplete evidence. The results of their work provide clear evidence that governments and families must invest more than the cost of school uniforms in attempts to improve the public school system.[19]

❖ DISCUSSION QUESTIONS

1. Why do you think there are more people who would indicate on a survey that they are affiliated with a religion than there are people who attend religious services on a regular basis?

2. Before you read this chapter, did you know the names of your senators and representative? Did you know their party affiliations? Why or why not? Why is it important to know who they are and how they vote?

3. What do you think the purpose of *public* schools should be? Do you think your education fulfilled that purpose? Why or why

not? Did you go to public schools in primary and secondary schools? Why or why not?

4. Do you think religious symbols should be allowed in public schools? Why or why not?

5. Do you ever wonder why the word "God" is used so often by public officials in their public statements? Discuss why you think this happens.

6. How might the government, religious, and educational institutions work together to improve the situation of those who rioted during the 2005 riots in France?

7. Do you think that the French government needs to recognize the religious, racial, and ethnic diversity within France? If yes, why? (And how might the government go about doing so?) If not, why not?

❖ SUGGESTIONS FOR SPECIFIC ACTIONS

1. Go to http://www.house.gov/. Find one issue up for debate in the House of Representatives that interests you. Research the issue and write a letter to your representative to encourage him or her to vote your way.

2. Attend two different types of religious services in your local community. Observe and compare what types of people are in positions of authority (their gender, race, and age). Think about how these different religious groups might influence society if they were the "official" state religions.

3. Research a religious organization that is working on a social justice issue. Write a two-page essay outlining the scope of the issue, why the organization is addressing the issue, and how they are carrying out their campaign (what methods they are using). Include at least one paragraph analyzing the power that religious groups can have in organizing citizens toward a more just society. Finally, determine how you can help with their campaign and follow through with at least one action to do so. Here are some possible campaigns that might interest you:

AFSC's anti-War in Iraq campaign: http://www.afsc.org/iraq/

Mazon's anti-hunger campaign: http://www.mazon.org

Church World Service's Sudan campaign: http://www.church worldservice.org/news/Sudan/

4. These are just a few examples; you should feel free to come up with your own as well!

Please go to our Web site at http://www.sagepub.com/korgen to find further civic engagement opportunities, resources, and peer-reviewed articles related to this chapter.

❖ ENDNOTES

1. The pledge, originally written in 1892, was amended in 1923, 1924, and 1954. The phrase "under God" was the most recent addition, added during the Cold War in part to distinguish the United States from the USSR, which had outlawed religious practice.

2. See Gary Becker's "Human Capital and Poverty." Accessed at http://www.acton.org/publicat/randl/article.php?id=258 on November 14, 2005.

3. See the federal government's No Child Left Behind Act Web site at http://www.ed.gov/nclb/landing.jhtml.

4. A U.S. District Court ruled that the school board's decision to mandate the teaching of intelligent design violated the constitutional separation between church and state. See Associated Press 2005.

5. National Public Radio 2005.

6. The government's failure to fulfill this responsibility during and after Hurricane Katrina in 2005 was (and continues to be) painfully displayed. Hundreds of Americans lost their lives and millions more lost their homes, livelihoods, and neighborhoods, due to the breach that occurred in the levees protecting New Orleans.

7. Of the remaining, 3.7% affiliated themselves with other religious groups (these groups consist of those with which less than .03% of the population affiliated themselves) and 5.4% refused to answer the question.

8. Keysar, Ariela, Barry A. Kosmin, and Egon Mayer. 2001. "American Religious Identification Survey." Accessed at http://www.gc.cuny.edu/faculty/research_briefs/aris/aris_index.htm on November 13, 2005.

9. According to George Gallup, Jr., "a representative global village of 1000 would include: 300 Christians (183 Catholics, 84 Protestants, 33 Orthodox), 175 Muslims, 128 Hindus, 55 Buddhists, 47 Animists, 210 without any professed religion, and 85 from miscellaneous religious groups"

(Gallup, George, Jr. 1996. Foreign Policy Research Institute [FPRI] Wire "Religion and Civic Virtue at Home and Abroad." *The Templeton Lecture on Religion and World Affairs* 4[1]).

10. Bottomore 1964:27.

11. It is important to note that Marx was not exposed to religions that actively promoted social justice as many have done in the past century. In recent years, some religious leaders (like Liberation Theologians) have been accused of being Marxists!

12. Young 2002:661.

13. "Religion in the World at the End of the Millennium." Accessed at http://www.gallup-international.com/ContentFiles/millennium15.asp on November 12, 2005.

14. The Bill of Rights Institute's Web site is located at http://www .billofrightsinstitute.org/instructional/resources/LandMarkSupremeCourt Cases/#ReligionEst

15. To see the Supreme Court's full opinion of this case, go to the Legal Information Institute Supreme Court Collection, found at http://straylight .law.cornell.edu/supct/html/99-62.ZS.html on November 14, 2005.

16. Bell 2005.

17. Cesari 2005.

18. Brunsma and Rockquemore 1998.

19. To learn more about the issue of school uniforms, read Brunsma's *The School Uniform Movement and What it Tells Us About American Education: A Symbolic Crusade* (Scarecrow Press, 2004).

❖ REFERENCES

Associated Press. 2005. "Judge Rules Against Intelligent Design." MSNBC, December 20th. Accessed at http://www.msnbc.msn.com/id/10545387/ on March 14, 2006.

Bell, Susan. 2005. "French Curfew Will Keep Rioters Off Streets." *The Scotsman* Web site, November 9. Accessed at http://news.scotsman.com/interna tional.cfm?id=2215032005 on November 20, 2005.

Bottomore, Thomas, trans. and ed. 1964, *Karl Marx: Early Writings.* New York: McGraw-Hill, p. 27.

Brunsma, David L. and Kerry A. Rockquemore. 1998. "Effects of Student Uniforms on Attendance, Behavior Problems, Substance Use, and Academic Achievement." *Journal of Educational Research* 92(1), Sep/Oct: 53–63.

Brunsma, David. 2004. *The School Uniform Movement and What It Tells Us About American Education: A Symbolic Crusade.* Lanham, MD: Scarecrow Press.

Cesari, Jocelyne. 2005. "Ethnicity, Islam, and *les banlieues*: Confusing the Issues." Social Science Research Council Web site "Riots in France." Accessed at http://riotsfrance.ssrc.org/Cesari/ on March 14, 2006.

National Public Radio (NPR). 2005. "Teaching Evolution: A State by State Debate." Accessed at http://www.npr.org/templates/story/story.php?storyId=4630737 on March 14, 2006.

Young, Michael P. 2002. "Confessional Protest: The Religious Birth of U.S. National Social Movements." *American Sociological Review* 67(5): 660–88.

8

Deviant Behavior and Social Movements

W hat would be your reaction if you saw a man dressed in knee length pants, wearing a wig, or snorting tobacco? Would you think his behavior deviant? Probably! However, sniffing tobacco and wearing a wig and breeches were once considered normal. In fact, in colonial America, engaging in such behavior demonstrated high social status. Our understanding of what is deviant behavior is socially constructed and changes over time and from society to society.

Although behaviors such as incest and killing innocent people are considered deviant in almost all societies, much else of what is considered deviant behavior varies across cultures and time periods. Notions of what constitutes deviant behavior can also be situational. There are circumstances in which acts that would normally be considered completely beyond the bounds of acceptable behavior, including many brutal acts of violence, can come to be seen as normal and appropriate. For example, soldiers' reports and memoirs frequently include accounts of acts that may seem unjustifiable once the fighting has ended but which seemed acceptable, even necessary, in the midst of it. This chapter will discuss (a) how deviance is defined, (b) how the three major theoretical perspectives view deviance, (c) why some social groups are labeled as deviant, and (d) how some social movements have changed society by "normalizing" certain deviant behavior.

As you will recall from Chapter Four, cultural norms are socially constructed expectations for behavior. A society's norms include basic behaviors, manners and etiquette, laws and legal code, and the society's unique culture and ways of doing things. As members of a society, we learn which behaviors are appropriate through socialization. Our actions are guided by how we see others behave, how we are taught by our socializing agents to behave, and by the reactions of those with whom we interact.

Folkways are norms that are enforced through informal *rewards* and *sanctions* (such as approval or disapproval from others). For example, we follow folkways when we hold the door for someone following us, let people we speak with finish their sentences without interruption, and make conversation with people we meet at parties. Violating these folkways might result in a dirty look or being considered rude, socially awkward, or strange. However, this type of deviant behavior hardly ever results in serious social repercussions and never results in legal repercussions.

Mores, on the other hand, are those norms that relate to behaviors that reflect the values that society holds most dear. For example, refusing to support a colleague in need, cheating on a girlfriend or boyfriend, or openly announcing you are bisexual often results in people expressing strong reactions that can have negative repercussions (e.g., being labeled as "not a team player" at work, as untrustworthy and selfish by friends, or being thought of as sexually abnormal by some).

The most powerful mores, those representing our deepest values, are called *taboos.* Incest, sexual relations between close family members, is a taboo in almost all societies. Cannibalism, the practice of eating humans, is also widely considered to be a taboo. Those who carry out such acts are regarded as socially repugnant and face widespread, if not universal, condemnation from the other members of their society.

Laws are norms that are formalized rules of behavior enacted by legislatures and enforced by formal sanctions carried out by the criminal and civil justice systems. Laws provide guidelines as to what people should do (e.g., drivers should stop at stop signs, citizens should pay taxes, parents should send their children to school) and what people should *not* do (e.g., commit rape, robbery, insurance fraud, or possess or use certain drugs). Those who break laws are subject to fines, imprisonment, and even, possibly, death.

Exercise 8.1   Nonverbal Sanctions

Next time you see someone give a nonverbal, negative sanction (a look of disgust, a gasp, or some other nonverbal sign of disapproval), ask yourself the following questions:

1. What norm is being broken (why did someone gasp, give a look of disgust, or carry out whatever nonverbal negative sanction they gave)?

2. What was the reaction of the norm-violator to the negative sanction?

3. What was your reaction to the interaction you witnessed between the norm violator and the person giving the negative sanction?

4. Why do you think you reacted this way? How did your own socialization process influence your reaction?

Exercise 8.2   Violating Norms and Food Waste

Often, we are so used to following the norms of society, that we forget that we *could* behave differently. Harold Garfinkel, a sociologist most famous for his "breaching" experiments whereby people would break folkways in order to expose them, had students do such things as act like boarders in their parent's homes, offer to pay store clerks less or more money than the price indicated on an item in a store, and question every statement a person makes in a conversation with them.[1] Through these experiments, his students challenged the norms of social interaction and, in the process, brought them to light.

Conduct your own breaching experiment on campus by carrying out the following steps:

1. Go to the End Hunger Network Web site at http://www.endhunger .com/. Find five facts about hunger in the United States and memorize them.

2. Go to your school cafeteria and fill your tray.

3. Eat about half of what's on your tray.

4. Bring your leftovers to the person managing the cafeteria, tell him or her the five facts you memorized about hunger in the United States, and ask him or her how you can make sure what you didn't eat goes to someone in the community who is hungry.

(Continued)

(Continued)

5. Go back to the End Hunger Network Web site at http://www.end hunger.com/. Click on "childhood hunger" and then "how to end it."

6. Write a 3–4 page paper that describes the following:

   a. what norms you violated with this experiment

   b. how the cafeteria manager (and anyone else who witnessed or was part of the conversation) reacted to you breaking those norms

   c. how doing this experiment made you feel (if you felt uncomfortable, explain why you did and how you handled those feelings)

   d. what students, in general, can do to help address the issue of childhood hunger and how your campus cafeteria can play a role

   e. what you, as an individual, can do to help address the issue of childhood hunger (based on what you learned on the End Hunger Network Web site)

❖ FUNCTIONALISM AND DEVIANCE

Emile Durkheim established the functionalist perspective on deviance.[2] He maintained that deviance and deviants actually serve several useful and necessary purposes, or functions, for society. Deviants can help to make the norms of society clearer to the majority population, unite the nondeviant members of society, and even promote social change.

Sometimes it is difficult to know what the norms of society are until we see someone punished for violating one. When some members of society are punished for committing deviant acts, the rules of society are clarified and reinforced for everyone. For example, seeing someone pulled over for speeding usually makes other drivers slow down. Observing a classmate punished for plagiarism helps students recognize that stealing someone else's words or ideas is unacceptable behavior and that those who do so are liable to be punished. It is not that you did not already know that speeding and plagiarism are wrong, but seeing these mores violated reminds us of how important it is to abide by these rules and often (if even only through fear of being punished) causes us to act as society wishes.

According to Durkheim, deviants can also unify members of society. When people see deviant behavior as a threat, they come together to punish and root out the deviant members of society. For example, in the mid-1990s, parishioners of St. Patrick's parish in Brockton, Massachusetts, became closely united when they organized to confront a prostitution and drug operation headquartered in abandoned buildings across the street from the church. The criminal activity centering on the abandoned buildings made them fearful when they came to the church, and they were tired of being afraid. They knew they really had to do something when the pastor was propositioned by a prostitute on the way to Mass! Working together, they compelled the city to take over the houses (in lieu of back taxes owed), raze them, and drive out those using them to commit deviant acts that made parishioners fear going to church. The experience brought the parishioners closer together as they learned they could rely on one another and become a powerful force when united.

The American people's response to the devastating effects of Hurricane Katrina in 2005 is another example of this positive function of deviant behavior. The *immediate* reaction of almost all Americans to the destruction it wreaked was to contribute what they could to relief efforts. Individuals, and even whole cities (such as Houston), opened their arms to fellow Americans displaced by the hurricane and the failure of the levees.

Durkheim also maintained that deviants promote social change in society. He believed that societies would stagnate if they did not change and that all social change begins with deviance.[3] Laws that do more harm than good for society must be violated. Society needs people willing to break them. United States and world history is replete with examples of deviants, such as women fighting for equal rights, American revolutionaries (before the war for independence was won), and civil rights leaders, who became heroes by protesting and helping to overturn unjust laws and governments. For example, Mildred Jeter, a Black woman, and Richard Loving, a White man, were considered criminals when they married in 1958, in violation of the law in their state of Virginia, which prohibited interracial marriage. However, their actions resulted in the 1967 Supreme Court Decision (Loving v. Virginia) that declared such laws unconstitutional and led to a tremendous increase in the number of interracial marriages in the United States.

❖ CONFLICT THEORY AND DEVIANCE

As you will recall from Chapter Two, Marxist and other conflict theorists maintain that society is made up of groups competing for power. In turn, they believe that norms and laws are largely created by and for the benefit of those who hold the most power in society. Marx argued that the members of the ruling class (the owners of the means of production) use every instrument at their disposal, including shaping norms and laws, to protect their interests. Therefore, the actions of the poor are more likely to be labeled as deviant and criminal than those of rich individuals or major corporations.

In *The Rich Get Richer and the Poor Get Prison*,[4] Jeffrey Reiman uses the conflict perspective[5] to argue that the criminal justice system is biased against poor people and in favor of wealthy individuals and corporations. He maintains that corporations actually do much more harm to society by committing acts that are not officially labeled "criminal" than individuals do who commit acts that are considered crimes. For example, preventable injuries and deaths resulting from or caused by unsafe workplaces (e.g., black lung disease, asbestos-based cancer, repetitive motion injuries, cave-ins in coal mines), unsafe medical practices (e.g., unnecessary surgeries, lack of proper medical care, drug interactions), environmental pollution (e.g., cigarettes, pollution from chemical and industrial factories), and lax oversight of consumer safety (e.g., defective tires, tainted meat) harm far more people than criminal acts carried out by individuals. However, they are largely ignored by the judicial system and the media, whereas the crimes of predominantly poor and minority citizens are portrayed as a great threat to society. This skewed portrayal of deviance makes people feel most threatened from below (poor, predominantly minority people) rather than above (wealthy individuals and corporations).

❖ SYMBOLIC INTERACTIONISM AND DEVIANCE

Symbolic interactionists maintain that people learn to conform or deviate from the norms of society through their interactions with others. They stress that deviance is socially constructed and that deviant behavior is learned. Two of the most well-known theories on deviance that fall under the umbrella of the symbolic interactionist perspective are Differential Association Theory and Labeling Theory.

Through his Differential Association Theory,[6] Donald Sutherland maintains that people learn deviant behavior by associating with people who commit deviant acts. That is, people tend to base their own behavior on how they see those they interact with behaving. Therefore, those who are raised in families that violate social norms or spend much of their time with friends who break the norms of society will be more likely than others to act in deviant ways.

Labeling Theory, another symbolic interactionist perspective on deviance, focuses on the categorization of people as deviant. Howard Becker,[7] the founder of Labeling Theory, maintains that behavior and individuals only *become* deviant when people with some social power label them as deviant. Once people so labeled accept this categorization, they begin to consider themselves deviant and act accordingly. For example, when a person becomes known to others as a drug addict, ostracized by those who do not use illegal drugs, and given the label "druggie," she begins to socialize more and more with fellow "druggies" and act like the "druggie" people perceive her to be. We can see the effects of this on high school campuses when kids who have been labeled as "outcasts" begin to take on the qualities of that label, sometimes with violent results.

❖   LABELING SOME SOCIAL GROUPS AS DEVIANT

As noted above, deviance is a *social construction*, which means that behaviors are not by themselves normal or deviant; they only become deviant when society defines them as such. Unfortunately, it is easy and common to define or perceive entire groups of people as deviant people, rather than merely defining specific behaviors as deviant acts. For instance, the practice of subjecting people to greater scrutiny, or treating some people as potentially dangerous, based on stereotypes and prejudices associated with their perceived race is called *racial profiling*.

The state of New Jersey became a focal point for a national debate on racial profiling in the 1990s. Black motorists complained, and an independent review confirmed, that they were being pulled over for routine traffic stops, and even searches, far more often than members of other racial and ethnic groups, and often without cause.[8] A whole new term has entered our collective lexicon to describe this unfair treatment, "Driving While Black." A series of reviews, including a number of hearings in the State Senate, followed, resulting in the establishment of guidelines for law enforcement officers that point out that "any officer can unwittingly or subconsciously fall prey to racial or ethnic stereotypes about who is more likely to be involved in criminal activity" and mandate that officers work to counter this fact by focusing on people's conduct rather than their racial or ethnic appearance.[9]

Police and other law enforcement agencies have many forms of profiling at their disposal, most of which focus on behavior. A Rand Corporation commentary, "Racial Profiling: Lessons from the Drug

War"[10] criticizes racial profiling as ineffective. The report advocates "tactical profiling," which would focus on behaviors rather than identities, and which would look for reasons *not* to suspect people when making otherwise random stops and searches, rather than emphasizing reasons to target people.[11]

❖ ORGANIZING FOR CHANGE

It is useful for the well-being and maintenance of society to construct norms and to recognize forms of deviance. Without these, we would need to be consistently navigating the basic rules of behavior and contact in every situation we enter. How inefficient and chaotic that would be! However, social norms that reinforce the worldviews and interests of dominant groups (those in power) often act as repressive forces against the worldviews and interests of minority groups and all of those who would choose to deviate (even in harmless ways) against the dominant culture. Furthermore, once a perspective takes on the veneer of "reality" or "truth" or "the right way," it is difficult to change it. Only concerted, organized effort can effectively counter such social forces. And the history of the United States is a history of people doing just that, coming together to create the changes they desire for society.

Before the Civil Rights Movement, for example, segregation laws throughout the country prohibited Black Americans from using the same facilities or drinking from the same water fountains as White Americans. Under "separate but equal" laws, Black Americans were relegated to inferior schools. Under "Jim Crow" laws in the South, Black people were harassed when attempting to vote; some were the victims of violence, and others were simply turned away without being allowed to cast their votes. Jim Crow laws also put a large variety of other restrictions on Black people that limited their ability to operate as White Americans could. Anyone breaking these laws was considered deviant and deserving of legal punishment. It took many decades of struggle, culminating in the Civil Rights Movement of the 1950s and 1960s, to make opposing racism a socially approved, rather than a deviant, act.

Rosa Parks, famous for her bus boycott during the Civil Rights Movement, was not the only Black person arrested in 1955 for violating segregation laws, but hers was the perfect "test case" to take to the Supreme Court. She was poised, respectable, and fully prepared for the negative publicity. "People always say that I didn't give up my seat because I was tired, but that isn't true," Rosa Parks wrote.

"No, the only tired I was, was tired of giving in."[12] Parks, an elected officer of the local chapter of the NAACP (National Association for the Advancement of Colored People), had been part of the group of activists strategizing the best way to challenge the segregation laws, not just in court, but in public awareness. She had not planned on getting arrested that day, but when she was told to move, she recognized the opportunity. By allowing herself to be taken off the bus by police, she provided the spark for a campaign that had already started to challenge the laws that made Black Americans second-class citizens.

The activists formed the Montgomery Improvement Association, a coalition of local groups, including several church organizations, whose purpose was to demand the desegregation of buses without appearing to be too radical or threatening. A young pastor with no known enemies or personal agenda, Dr. Martin Luther King, Jr., was selected to head the campaign. Despite the hardships that poor people faced getting to work each day without public transportation, threats from motorists as they walked along the roads, and warnings that they would lose their jobs if they could not get to work each day on time, the Black citizens of Montgomery organized themselves effectively and boycotted the buses for more than a year. By the time they won their case in court, they had also fostered a national reexamination of the status of Black people in America. Although African Americans still face routine de facto segregation, discrimination, and insults, the Montgomery bus boycott is credited with tearing down the laws that supported and "normalized" such actions.

Exercise 8.3	Lunch Counter Sit-Ins and Nonviolent Protest

One of the more dramatic forms of protest of the Civil Rights Movement was the "lunch counter sit-in." In these events, Blacks took seats at lunch counters that only served Whites, and then refused to leave. During many of these sit-ins, White customers jeered at them, threw food at them, and threatened them, before the police came and dragged them off.

Use your library's databases (we suggest you use the JSTOR database) to find three academic articles that focus on lunch counter sit-ins during the Civil Rights Movement. Also, watch the first chapter of the "Eyes on the Prize" documentaries (your school library should have a copy), in which the sit-ins are covered. Then, write a 2–3 page paper that addresses the following questions:

(Continued)

(Continued)

1. Given the fact that the protesters knew they were not going to be served, what did they hope to gain by doing this? Were they trying to change the law? Public opinion? The policies of the lunch counter establishments?

2. Do you think their strategy was successful? What are the benefits and positives of nonviolent protest? What are the negatives and limitations?

3. Consider public opinion today toward Black Americans.
   a. What sorts of public actions could Black Americans do today to bring attention to the kinds of discrimination they face?

   b. What actions can you, personally, take that would help diminish racial discrimination?

Hand in a complete bibliography of your sources along with your written answers. Look through the following Web site to make sure that you are using proper American Sociological Association citations: http://www .calstatela.edu/library/bi/rsalina/asa.styleguide.html

Exercise 8.4   Advising a Social Movement

There have been numerous social movements in the United States (organized campaigns for social, cultural, or legal change) that have met varying degrees of success over the past 50 years. The cultural period known as "the sixties" (roughly 1963–73) saw the rise of the second wave of the Women's Movement,[13] the American Indian Movement, the Brown Power Movement (Latinos), an anti-war movement (Vietnam), movements for poverty relief and fair housing practices, gay rights, animal rights, environmental rights, and an international student–youth movement, among others.

Pick one of these movements and answer the following questions. Use your library's databases and search for articles using such keywords as "American Indian Movement," and "organization, successes, failures, media, portrayal," and "goals."

1. What were or are the goals of the movement?

2. How was or is the movement organized? How was or is it run? How is or was it viewed in the popular media? How do you think the movement was or is organized and how has its portrayal in the media affected its ability to achieve its goals?

3. How successful or unsuccessful has the movement been (or was it) in achieving its goals?

4. Imagine you were hired as a consultant to promote and advise the movement. What would you do or say to help it achieve its goals? Be specific and strategic, outlining plans to carry forth your proposal.

Exercise 8.5   Campus Activism: Then and Now

The 1960's were famous for student activism and student organizing. Who were these students, and for what were they advocating? How were they portrayed in the news media at the time? How are they being portrayed by the media and history textbooks today? How successful were they? Can you imagine similar types of student activism taking place on your campus today? Are there any? Write a 3–4 page paper that answers these questions by carrying out the following steps:

1. Go to the newspaper archive in your library.

2. Choose either one regional or national paper for which there are issues available from 1963–1973.

3. Read through issues published between 1963 and 1973 until you have located (and photocopied) at least 10 articles about on-campus student activism.

4. For each article, note the following:

   a. Does the article tell you what the students wanted?

   b. Does the article tell you why they had those goals?

   c. Does the article appear to have a position in support of, neutral to, or opposed to the students?

   d. For each case in which you have a clear sense of the students' goals, were they achieved? Did they change society?

5. Can you see sixties-style student protests happening today on your campus? If yes, would the protesters have similar or different goals than the protesters from the sixties that you read about? If no, explain why you think they would not take place today. Have other styles of protest replaced them? Have students become less likely to protest and, if so, why?

Exercise 8.6   Test Yourself

We all know something about explicit racism or sexism and deliberate discrimination. But many of our prejudices are implicit—hidden in our own assumptions about how the world works and in the associations we make. For example, you might believe that women should have the same opportunities as men in the workplace, but you still might think, consciously or subconsciously, that male workers seeking promotion exhibit better "leadership qualities" than the female workers. Where did your ideas about "leadership" come from, and how are they associated with gender?

1. Visit Project Implicit at https://implicit.harvard.edu/implicit/ Select the "Research" option; read all of the orientation information, and register.

2. Take one of the tests. Some of the tests measure associations that are unrelated to this chapter. If you are given one of those, either take it or not as you wish, but then return until you are placed in a related test.

3. Complete the entire evaluation, as honestly as possible, until you reach the one page assessment at the end. Read and save that page. Do not hand it in.

4. Did anything surprise you about your assessment? Were any of the questions difficult for you? Did answering them raise any questions or concerns for you?

Write a 1–2 page paper explaining when or how you might unintentionally discriminate against someone due to the associations you make between characteristics of people that you perceive and characteristics that you cannot perceive (but assume). This may be a difficult task, so press yourself to really dig deep in uncovering your hidden prejudices and acts of discrimination.

Sociologist in Action: Eileen O'Brien

Many students, especially White male students, are often reluctant to study racial and other types of inequality in their sociology courses because they feel that these courses "blame White men"—that is, they interpret the macro statistical data that often show White men at the top of the stratification ladder on almost every sociodemographic indicator to mean that they are somehow "at fault" for everyone else being lower down. While it is true that we usually find White men at the top of the U.S. stratification ladder, this is certainly not a unanimous pattern, nor does it mean that everyone in this category is directly "at fault" for the situation. Sociologist Eileen O'Brien's research uses qualitative data to examine what Melanie Bush calls "cracks in the wall of Whiteness"—that is, micro dynamics of racial inequality in which the dominance of Whiteness is challenged. These "cracks" allow us to discover ways that social systems could be restructured to reflect a more egalitarian society.

For example, O'Brien's book *Whites Confront Racism* studies White antiracist activists who "daily, vigilantly challenge White supremacy." She interviewed these activists to determine what factors in their life combined to motivate them to work toward ending racism and created a typology of strategies that Whites typically use to confront racism. O'Brien regularly gives workshops in various settings (such as local public school districts and universities) for individuals of all racial backgrounds seeking ways to interrupt and confront racism in their daily lives and in the institutions where they live and work. These workshops present strategies that O'Brien gleaned from the activists she studied. O'Brien also profiled two major antiracist organizations, Anti-Racist Action and People's Institute for Survival and Beyond, to demonstrate how social movement organizations shape and define the problem (in this case, racism) for their participants in ways that affect their respective strategies. O'Brien chose to donate 100% of her share of the profits from the sale of her book to these two organizations to assist them in their efforts.

O'Brien has also found cracks in the wall of Whiteness in other places. For example, her work with sociologist Joe Feagin in *White Men on Race* examines upper-income White men's racial attitudes. Economically privileged White men differ from middle America in that they do not typically deny that racism exists and that they usually are aware when racism occurs in their midst. However, they typically do not use their powerful positions to confront it as they should; confronting the perpetrators would mean that they would disturb their comfortable and profitable relationships with others in their strata. O'Brien and Feagin describe this dynamic as the "White dysfunctional family," and recommend public policy strategies for breaking the pattern in their book. O'Brien's current research project involves interviews with Latinos and Asian Americans who have found enough cracks in the wall of Whiteness to permeate it and even consider themselves White, in various ways. She seeks to demonstrate how Whiteness's seemingly rigid walls are actually quite flexible when it comes to certain ethnic groups and to uncover the circumstances under which this flexibility occurs.

❖ DISCUSSION QUESTIONS

1. What was the last norm that you broke? Think of the last folk-way (rather than a more) that you violated. What was the reaction of those around you? How did it make you feel? Did the reaction impact your willingness to break the folkway in the future?

2. Have you ever broken a rule or law that you considered unjust? Why did you do so? Did you organize your deviant behavior with other people or did you violate the norm on your own? What were the repercussions? Did it result in any lasting social change? Why or why not?

3. The U.S. Department of Homeland Security asks us to report "suspicious activities" to law enforcement agencies. On the agency Web site (http://www.ready.gov), former Secretary Tom Ridge says that "overcoming terrorism requires . . . the vigilance of every American." What activities are we supposed to be looking for? What do you think makes a behavior "suspicious" enough to report to the police? What, if any, might be the negative implications of members of the public viewing each other as suspects?

4. What are the norms that guide your classroom behavior? What would you consider deviant classroom behavior by students? How did you learn these norms? What are the sanctions for those who violate classroom norms?

5. What do you think are the greatest threats to our society? Why do you think we are more likely to hear news reports about a murder or robbery than about the deaths caused by lack of access to adequate medical care and toxic pollutants?

6. What do you think life would be like without norms? Would it be possible? Why or why not?

7. Think of some examples that support Durkheim's idea that deviance can serve positive functions for society. Now think of how deviance can have a negative influence on society. What are the situations in which deviance is most likely to have (a) a positive or (b) a negative effect on society?

❖ SUGGESTIONS FOR SPECIFIC ACTIONS

1. Do something about racial profiling.

   a. Download the Amnesty International "Racial Profiling Action Kit" at http://www.amnestyusa.org/racial_profiling/pdf/Racial_Profiling_Action_Kit.pdf

   b. Choose one of the actions, or modify one of the actions to suit your interest. Get your instructor's approval before beginning your project. Actions may be local or national, educational or political. Keep a journal of your project, its outcome, feedback you get from others, and what you have learned by doing it.

2. Identify a social issue that you support. (Consider movements to regulate globalization, expand civil rights, define gay rights or gay marriage, oppose gay rights or gay marriage, protect foreign workers, register and interrogate foreign workers, etc.) Find a campus or local organization that works on this issue. Attend meetings and participate in the activities of the organization. Write a letter to the campus newspaper explaining to your classmates what the issues are that the group is concerned with, how these issues affect students, how the group is trying to change people's opinions and feelings on this issue, and why they should join the organization, too!

Please go to our Web site at http://www.sagepub.com/korgen to find further civic engagement opportunities, resources, and peer-reviewed articles related to this chapter.

❖ ENDNOTES

1. Garfinkel 1967.
2. Durkheim [1895] 1982.
3. Durkheim [1895] 1982.
4. Reiman 2003.
5. Among other theories about deviance and social control.
6. Sutherland 1947.
7. Becker 1963.
8. Lamberth 1994.

9. New Jersey Division of Criminal Justice.

10. Riley 2002.

11. Riley 2002.

12. Parks and Haskins 1992.

13. The first wave of the Women's Movement began in 1848 and ended with the passage of the 19th Amendment in 1920.

❖ REFERENCES

Becker, Howard. 1963. *Outsiders: Studies in the Sociology of Deviance.* New York: Free Press.

Durkheim, Emile. [1895] 1982. *The Rules of the Sociological Method.* Edited by Steven Lukes; translated by W. D. Halls. New York: Free Press.

Garfinkel, Harold. 1967. *Studies in Ethnomethodology.* Englewood Cliffs, NJ: Prentice Hall.

Lamberth, John. 1994. "Revised Statistical Analysis of the Incidence of Police Stops and Arrests of Black Drivers/Travelers on the New Jersey Turnpike Between Interchanges 1 and 3 from the Years 1988 through 1991." Accessed at http://www.lamberthconsulting.com/downloads/new_jersey_study_report.pdf on January 11, 2006.

New Jersey Division of Criminal Justice. 2005. "Overview of New Jersey's Racial Profiling Policy." Accessed at http://www.state.nj.us/lps/dcj/agguide/directives/racial-profiling/pdfs/overview-racial-policy.pdf on January 1, 2006.

Parks, Rosa and James Haskins. 1992. *Rosa Parks: My Story.* New York: Dial Books.

Reiman, Jeffrey. 2003. *The Rich Get Richer and the Poor Get Prison: Ideology, Class and Criminal Justice.* Boston: Allyn and Bacon.

Riley, K. Jack. 2002. "Racial Profiling: Lessons From the Drug War." In *Rand Review* 26(2), Summer. Accessed at http://www.rand.org/publications/randreview/issues/rr.08.02/profiling.html on January 11, 2006.

Sutherland, Donald. 1947. *Principles of Criminology.* 4th ed. Philadelphia: J. B. Lippincott.

9

Big Money Doesn't *Always* Win

Stratification

Money, money, money . . .

It's a rich man's world[1]

Do you agree with the lyrics to this ABBA song? Do you think "It's a rich man's world"? In this chapter, we examine *social stratification,* how societies distribute the things valued in their society and rank groups of people according to their access to what is valued. Although people may prize certain things more in some societies than others (e.g., privacy, tea or coffee, certain spices, etc.), almost everyone, everywhere, highly values money.

As we discussed in Chapter Six, corporate-dominated globalization has spread across the world. In its wake, inequality has increased, as access to money is exploited by the already wealthy and denied to many of the poor and working classes. In the United States, the top

1% of households now own more wealth than *all* of the bottom 90% combined! Income and wealth inequality have not been this uneven since before the Great Depression hit in 1929. According to the Federal Reserve Board, this trend is only increasing. Between 2001 and 2004, the wealth of the bottom 40% of the population fell while the wealth of the top 10% increased.[2]

The growing gap between the rich and poor affects everyone in some way. As the gap widens, the social distance between rich and poor increases, and it becomes harder for those who have little to attain more. Today, those who hope to gain jobs that pay well must have (a) a high level of education, (b) connections to those in power, or (c) both.

❖ THEORIES OF SOCIAL STRATIFICATION

Classical Theories

Of the three main theories we discuss in the book (Functionalism, Conflict Theory, and Symbolic Interactionism), the consensus among sociologists is that Conflict Theory is the most useful when examining social stratification. The two founders of sociology who used the conflict perspective, Karl Marx and Max Weber, provided two of the most important classical theories of stratification. All of Marx's, and much of Weber's, work focused on examining and explaining inequality in society.

As you will recall from earlier chapters, Karl Marx spent his life examining how power is unequally distributed and how we might change society to make this distribution process fair. In most of his work, he maintained that there are only two classes in society: those who own the means of production (the owners, or bourgeoisie) and those who work for them (the workers, or proletariat). Marx believed that the workers would eventually realize that their interests are in opposition to those of the owners (in the process, forming a "class consciousness" for all laborers) and ultimately overthrow the owner class.

Weber, who lived a generation or so after Marx, expanded upon Marx's ideas.[3] Whereas Marx maintained that power in society directly relates to ownership of the means of production (those who own industries), Weber recognized that nonowners who possess useful skills can also have some power. He added a third class, a middle class, to Marx's two tiered class system. In doing so, he divided the nonowners into a middle class (those who had skills based on knowledge) and a working class (those who did manual labor). Weber maintained that as societies became more complicated and technologically advanced, the skills of the middle class would become more in demand than those of the working class. Those in the middle class would, therefore, be paid more and have greater access to the things valued in society (better schools, neighborhoods, housing, etc.) than the members of the working class. Unlike Marx, he didn't envision a class uprising that would result in the destruction of the owner class.

Contemporary Theories

Today, *power elite theories,* a modern offshoot of the classic conflict perspective, represent the dominant perspective in studies of economic and political power. Power elite theorists maintain that many people do not bother participating in the political process because they feel alienated from it. Power elite theorists, such as C. Wright Mills[4] and William Domhoff,[5] note that a relatively small, organized group of people hold key positions in the major institutions of society and make continuous (and, overall, successful) efforts toward keeping themselves in power.

Exercise 9.1   Social Welfare, Wealthfare, and Corporate Welfare

In his book, *The Structure of Social Stratification in the United States,* Leonard Beeghley argues that the middle class has struck a bargain with the upper class to maintain the present class system at the expense of the lower class.

- Go to the Web site for the Joint Committee on Taxation at http://www.house.gov/jct/.
- Click on the eagle (where it says "Click here to continue").
- Under the Table of Contents, go to Joint Committee on Taxation Publications.
- Click on "Joint Committee on Taxation Publications 2005."
- Click on "Estimates Of Federal Tax Expenditures For Fiscal Years 2005–2009."

(Continued)

(Continued)

1. According to the table titled "Estimates of Federal Tax Expenditures," what percentage of federal tax money is spent on (a) corporations, (b) wealthy individuals, (c) the middle class, and (d) poor Americans?

2. Do you think this is fair? Why or why not?

3. Do you think the way in which our tax money is allocated provides evidence for Beeghley's contention that the middle class and the upper class have agreed to benefit themselves at the expense of the poor? Why or why not?

❖ SOCIAL CLASS

What social class are you? Wait, we can guess (with at least 95% certainty) how you will answer! When asked on surveys, almost all Americans will say they are middle class. Most, however, have no social scientific understanding about what social class means. According to social scientists (those who measure class, professionally), people in the same class have relatively equal access to what is valued in our society (e.g., money, power, good schools, nice neighborhoods, etc.) and have similar lifestyles. Once people realize this, they can usually recognize the many differences concealed by the almost universal "middle class" label in the United States. For example, it quickly becomes clear that, whereas both high level managers and sales associates tend to refer to themselves as middle class, members of these respective occupations do not have similar lifestyles or access to what is valued in our society.

Because social scientists understand that almost all Americans will simply put down "middle class" if asked their social class, most measure social class by looking at the income, education, and profession of respondents. This still leaves some room for error.[6] In general, though, most truly middle class people have some college education, have professions with salaries (rather than jobs where they are paid by the hour) and earn within a specified range around the median income. Sometimes, social scientists break down members of the middle class into two groups: middle class (white collar workers) and working class (blue collar workers or pink collar workers[7]). Blue and pink collar jobs, which usually do not require as much education, tend to pay less than white collar work.[8] White collar work tends to require at least a bachelor's degree. The importance of attaining a college degree cannot be overstated. According to the Bureau of Labor Statistics,[9] in 2003 only 1.7% of those with college diplomas were among the working poor. However, 14.1% of persons with less than a high school diploma had jobs that did not lift them out of poverty (they are members of the *working* poor).

Gender and race are also factors that relate to social class. In short, it helps to be male and White. Female heads of households are twice as likely as male heads of families to be among the working poor.[10] In 2004, 11.5% of men and 13.9% of women were in poverty.[11] The poverty rate also varies dramatically according to race. In 2003, 8.2% of Whites, 24.4% of Blacks, 11.8% of Asians, 22.5% of Hispanics, and 23.2% of Alaskan Natives and American Indians lived in poverty.[12] We'll talk more about the connection between gender and race and social class in Chapters 10 and 11.

Exercise 9.2   Social Class and You

At this point in the chapter, you are probably thinking about your own social class and how you became a member of it. Think about how the institutions of family, education, and occupation are related to one another and answer the following questions:

1. What is the highest level of education completed by your parents?

2. Were you raised by two parents? If not, who raised you?

3. When you were growing up, what was the occupation of the head of your household?

4. How do you think your answers to questions 1–3 influenced your present social class?

5. Have you been in different social classes at different times in your life? If so, why? If not, why not?

❖ SOCIAL CLASS AND POLITICAL REPRESENTATION

Voter turnout is strongly related to social class. To put it simply, poor and working class people are much less likely to vote than middle class and wealthier Americans. Although always a feature of U.S. elections, the class gap has now become a "chasm." Those at the bottom of the income ladder are half as likely to vote as those at the top.[13] Many poor Americans do not see the issues that they care about being addressed by politicians and, therefore, see no use in going through the hassles of registering to vote and voting. Some are also too preoccupied with finding a way to pay the rent and buy food to think of much else. Homeless Americans, without proof of residence, have even more difficulty voting.

Exercise 9.3	Soup Kitchens and Hunger in America

Volunteer to serve a meal at an area soup kitchen. Your Campus Activities office should be able to help you and even connect you with a group on campus that regularly volunteers at the soup kitchen, or you can find one by using the National Hunger Clearinghouse Search Directory at http://www .worldhungeryear.org/nhc_data/nhc_01.asp.

1. Set up a time when the manager can give you some background on why the guests come to the soup kitchen (in particular, ask what makes them need the services the soup kitchen offers).

2. When you are there, be sure to pay attention to the guests eating at the soup kitchen and note the following:

    a. Are they mostly families or individuals?

    b. What is their racial–ethnic makeup?

    c. What is the age range of the guests?

    d. Do most seem hopeful? Resigned? Angry? Happy? Depressed?

3. Next, write a 2–3 page paper that describes

    a. the services the soup kitchen offers

    b. the demographics and attitudes of the people eating at the soup kitchen

    c. why the people who eat there need to do so

    d. how your experience at the soup kitchen made you feel

    e. whether or not you could ever see yourself needing the services of a soup kitchen (and why or why not)

Extra Credit: Go to the Web site for America's Second Harvest at http:// www.hungerinamerica.org/. Locate the most recent report and read the Executive Summary. Now, incorporate the statistics and analysis from this report into the paper you just wrote.

Increasing numbers of working class people have also become alienated from the political process. As Thomas Patterson, the author of *The Vanishing Voter*,[14] points out,

> The voting rate among those at the bottom of the income ladder is only half that of those at the top. [In the first half of the 20th century], working-class Americans were at the center of political debate and party conflict. They now occupy the periphery of a political world in which money and middle-class concerns are ascendant. In 2000, low-income respondents were roughly 30 percent more likely than those in the middle- or top-income groups to say the election's outcome would have little or no impact on their lives.[15]

According to the Bureau of Labor Statistics,[16] union membership has declined from 20.1% in 1983 to 12.5% in 2004. Thirty-six percent of government workers are members of unions but only 8% of workers in the private sector belong to a union (down from approximately 16% in 1983). As the power of unions has declined, so has the ability of the working class to have their economic interests addressed by politicians.[17]

Exercise 9.4   America: Who Votes?

1. Go to the U.S. Census Web page at http://www.census.gov/Press-Release/www/releases/archives/voting/004986.html

2. Read "U.S. Voter Turnout Up in 2004, Census Bureau Reports."

3. Compare voting rates by race and educational attainment.

4. Based on the information in this chapter, why do you think the respective groups are more or less likely to vote than other Americans? What does this tell you about the connections (or at least perceived connections) between wealth and power?

5. What steps do you think should be taken toward engaging nonvoting Americans enough so that they will register and vote?

Even Americans who do vote realize that only a very small percentage of the population has the means to run for high political office. The amount of money people must be able to raise to establish a legitimate campaign prohibits the vast majority of people from running for such positions. For example, during the 2004 Congressional elections, the average candidates running for the House of Representatives and the Senate raised, respectively, $574,213 and $2,569,694. On the presidential level, the numbers are even more staggering: Incumbent George W. Bush raised $367,228,801 during his campaign for reelection to the presidency in 2004.[18]

The overall result of our current electoral system[19] is that most poor and working class Americans do not vote. In turn, they are largely ignored by political officeholders who must respond to constituents who do vote and contributors who help them raise the vast sums of money needed to gain and maintain their positions. Fortunately, changes can be made to this system that would help to restore the public's faith that their votes really do matter.

Exercise 9.5   Campaign Finance Reform

Campaign reform efforts receive momentum every few years when scandals about political corruption make the headlines. Your representatives will no doubt be voting on campaign finance reform legislation in the near future. Check out the following three Web sites:

http://www.publicagenda.org/issues/frontdoor.cfm?issue_type=campaign_finance

http://www.citizen.org/congress/campaign/index.cfm

http://www.opensecrets.org/

and answer the following questions:

1. What recent political scandals have prompted the current proposed campaign finance reform legislation?

2. Do you think campaign finance reform is necessary? Why or why not?

3. What was the result of the most recently passed campaign finance reform legislation?

4. What do you think would most effectively level the electoral playing field? How might you help bring these changes about?

5. Of the different proposals that you have read, which makes most sense to you and can you offer even further suggestions?

❖ THE POWER OF ORGANIZED PEOPLE

The information above may sound depressing to anyone committed to true democracy in the United States. However, it is only part of the picture. Whereas civic organizations may not exist in the size and number they once did,[20] there are many grassroots political organizations successfully representing "common" Americans. Although we do not hear about their efforts all that often on the evening news, they are accomplishing the vital task of giving voice to poor and working class persons.

As discussed in *How Sociology Can Save Democracy*,[21] broad-based organizing associations (organizations of organizations, including churches, synagogues, mosques, nonprofits, parents associations, and unions) are civic groups that teach people to use a "sociological eye" and a "sociological imagination" as they train them to become effective citizens. These organizations train ordinary Americans to question the status quo, connect their personal problems to public issues, and hold politicians and business leaders accountable to the citizenry. While there are many of these organizations (the Industrial Areas Foundation, PICO, Direct Action and Research Training, Organizing and Leadership Training Center, and Gamaliel are some), they all organize for power. Their ability to organize gives them the power to act as a kind of mediating institution for those without organized money and negotiate effectively with those who have political and financial power.

The following description of the Industrial Areas Foundation (IAF), found on the organization's Web site, provides insight into the efforts of these types of organizations.

> The IAF is non-ideological and strictly non-partisan, but proudly, publicly, and persistently political. The IAF builds a political base within society's rich and complex third sector—the sector of voluntary institutions that includes religious congregations, labor locals, homeowner groups, recovery groups, parents associations, settlement houses, immigrant societies, schools, seminaries, orders of men and women religious, and others. And then the leaders use that base to compete at times, to confront at times, and to cooperate at times with leaders in the public and private sectors. (http://www.industrialareasfoundation.org 2004)

South Bronx Churches (SBC), an IAF affiliate comprised of eight Catholic and seventeen Protestant churches, also provides a good example of the power of organized people. During the 1980s, the South

Bronx burned. Largely abandoned by government and business leaders, drugs were everywhere, shootings were commonplace and arson was incessant. A turning point came when SBC members began to talk to one another about their fears, frustrations, and hopes concerning their neighborhoods. They realized that, alone, none of them could do much, but together they had the power to improve their community. Part of their multifaceted plan to revitalize the area was the "Nehemia Homes" project, the creation of 1,000 houses for poor, working class residents.[22]

SBC's effort to save the South Bronx was a long struggle that included public confrontations with powerful mayors of New York City (David Dinkins, Ed Koch, and Rudolph Guiliani) and huge efforts to raise money from business leaders. In the end, they won. SBC succeeded in raising millions of dollars and convincing the city of New York to donate land for the project. Today, low income, working New Yorkers own 1,000 homes where there were once just burned-out and decrepit buildings.

More importantly, this accomplishment inspired those who participated in the effort and the many more who benefited from it to become more active citizens. In an interview carried out in 2004,[23] Felix Santiago, a key SBC member in the "Nehemiah Homes" project described what the experience did for him.

> We own the community now! When we went around with the police in the van [identifying drug-dealing hotspots in the 1980s], we were kind of afraid. We thought that maybe the drug dealers were going to see us. But we were not afraid, together. Everywhere we go, from New York to Albany, from Albany back to Washington, we would carry our signatures with us and we would put them on the table and say, "These 100,000 people agree with our agenda for change."
>
> That made a big difference in our lives. We began to own more of the community. It's something you learn with South Bronx Churches. You don't fear anybody. You can stand in front of the President of the United States and you can talk to him like we are here. You have power. In 1986, I would have been afraid to sit down here and talk to you. I would say, no way, no way, you don't want to talk to me. But when you get picked to be a leader and own what you got, you have the right to represent the community.

Felix Santiago does not just have a new home and a revitalized neighborhood. He has become an empowered, knowledgeable, and effective citizen.

This kind of transformation is happening all over the United States. As of 2004, the IAF had 55 affiliates in 21 states, Canada, Germany, and the United Kingdom. They have helped to pass living wage bills (Texas, Arizona, New York City), funded thousands of new homes for low-income workers (New York City, Philadelphia, Baltimore, Washington, DC), established the successful Alliance School System (in areas throughout the west and southwest), and convinced lawmakers to enact legislation to carry out large scale blight removal and urban revitalization (New York City).[24] As noted above, the IAF is just one of many community-based organizations working to give power to organized people.

Exercise 9.6   Community Organizing

1. Find out what community-based organizing associations are operating in your area. You can do this by checking out the Web sites for national organizations (IAF, Gamaliel, PICO, etc.) and finding the respective affiliates in your state.

2. Attend a meeting of a local community organization and write a four-page paper that discusses (a) the issues upon which the organization is currently focusing, (b) how they decided upon those issues, and (c) their strategy as they work on those issues. Discuss how these three items relate to (a) the sociological eye and (b) the sociological imagination, and what suggestions you can make that might help them to be even more successful and powerful in accomplishing their mission.

Sociologist in Action: Frances Fox Piven

Frances Fox Piven is a sociologist who never ceases to use her sociological research to influence society. When awarded the 2003 American Sociological Association's "Award for the Public Understanding of Sociology," the Distinguished Professor of Political Science and Sociology at the Graduate School and University Center of the City University of New York was described as "a scholar who is equally at home in the university setting and the world of politics."[25] The author or coauthor of renowned sociological texts on the disenfranchisement and political power of poor Americans (e.g., *Regulating the Poor*, 1972 and 1993; *Poor People's*

(Continued)

(Continued)

Movements, 1977; *The New Class War*, 1982 and 1985; *Why Americans Don't Vote*, 1988; *Why Americans Still Don't Vote* 2000), she puts her knowledge into action in the political arena. For example, in the 1960's, she used her research to expand welfare benefits. Her efforts to enfranchise the poor led to the establishment of the National Voter Registration Act of 1993 (popularly known as the Motor Voter Act).[26] She has fought an unrelenting battle against the "Welfare Reform" initiated in 1996, and has been a consistent proponent for the politics of disruption and mass protest.

In a recent article, Piven describes her advice for democratic reform today in the following way:

> Yes, we should work on our agenda of democratic reforms, including a national right to vote, a national voter registration system, the implementation of the National Voter Registration Act, Election Day a holiday, nonpartisan election officials, and so on. But we have to do more. . . . The time when mass protest is possible will come. We should be ready and receptive, obdurate and bold. The hip-hop voter registration campaign had a slogan, "vote or die." They were on the right track.[27]

Piven is one of the boldest living sociologists. Importantly, she is a dedicated social scientist as well as an activist. She conducts good social scientific research that can be examined and critiqued objectively. Although not everyone, or even all sociologists, would agree with Piven's strategies for political action, many have been inspired by her efforts to make our society a democracy in which people of all classes are represented equally.

Exercise 9.7   Gender Inequality, Poverty, and Economic Development

1. Go to the United Nations Population Fund's "State of World Population 2005" report overview at http://www.unfpa.org/swp/2005/english/ch1/index.htm

2. As you read the summary, take notes about how (a) gender inequality, (b) education, and (c) poverty and hunger affect the economic development of nations.

3. When you've finished reading the summary, review your notes and write a 1–2 page paper that summarizes how (a) gender inequality, (b) education, and (c) poverty and hunger affect the economic development of nations.

❖ DISCUSSION QUESTIONS

1. Are you a knowledgeable, active, and effective citizen? What makes you think you are or are not? If you are, how did you become one? If you are not, what do you think would make you become one?

2. What opportunities do you have *right now* to influence how your (a) school, (b) community, and (c) nation operate? How many of these opportunities are you now using? Why?

3. Think of an issue you'd like to see addressed and conduct a power analysis of who controls the decisions about that issue and how you might influence them. For example, say you want your school to serve Fair Trade coffee on campus (if it does not already). Who decides what coffee the school buys to sell on campus? How might you convince them to switch to Fair Trade coffee?

4. What social class level do you think you will attain? Why?

5. Do you think our tax structure in the United States is generally fair? Why or why not? What might make it more equitable?

6. Have you ever worked (or are you now working) at a relatively low-wage hourly job? Why or why not?

7. What is your immediate reaction when you think of minimum or low-wage workers? Why?

8. Do you think unions are needed for low-wage workers? Why or why not?

9. What do you think your life would be like if you remained at a low-wage hourly job for the rest of your life? How would it affect who you might marry, what kind of family you will have, what kind of home you will live in, what you will do for entertainment, and so forth?

10. How do you think the college degree you are planning to get will affect your social class? Why?

❖ SUGGESTIONS FOR SPECIFIC ACTIONS

1. Find a local community organizing association in your area (You can do this by looking for "affiliated organizations" at the Web sites of the IAF, PICO, Gamaliel, and so forth). Contact the lead organizer and set up a meeting with him or her. Find out

what issues they are working on at this time. Offer to use your skills as a college student to conduct some basic research for the group to help them learn about the issues.

2. Go to the "Rock the Vote" Web site at http://www.rockthevote .com/partners_rock.php and follow the directions there on how to conduct a registration drive on your campus.

3. Go to United for a Fair Economy's Web site: http://www.faire conomy.org/activist/index.html. Look through the list of actions that they are working on. Join one of their letter writing campaigns, write one of the op-eds that they are looking for, or organize a teach-in at your home or school on a current issue related to stratification and the growing wealth divide.

Please go to our Web site at http://www.sagepub.com/korgen to find further civic engagement opportunities, resources, and peer-reviewed articles related to this chapter.

❖ ENDNOTES

1. Lyrics to "Money, Money, Money" by ABBA found at http://www.all lyrics.us/Abba/Abba-Live/Money-Money-Money/ on December 4, 2005.

2. Bucks et al. 2006.

3. See Max Weber, 1968. *Economy and Society.* Totowa, NJ: Bedminster Press.

4. Mills 1956.

5. Domhoff 1967,1983, 2002, 2005.

6. For instance, this doesn't take into account student loans, whether one has a spouse who is working outside the home, children to support, etc.

7. "Blue" collar work refers to manual unskilled or semiskilled labor, like that carried out by mechanics, plumbers, and factory workers. Pink collar work is unskilled or semiskilled work traditionally carried out by women in positions such as waitresses, clerks, secretaries, and florists.

8. In general, workers who belong to unions earn higher wages than those who do not. According to the Bureau of Labor Statistics, in 2005, the median weekly salary of full-time union workers was $801 while the median weekly salary of full-time non-union workers was $622.00. See "Union Members in 2005" at http://www.bls.gov/news.release/union2.t02.htm.

In general, skilled laborers earn higher wages than nonskilled blue collar workers. Some skilled blue collar workers even earn higher salaries than some white collar workers. For example, in 2004, the median salary of mental health workers was $36,630 and the median salary for electricians was $45,200. (See

"Occupational Employment Statistics survey by occupation, November 2004" at http://www.bls.gov/news.release/ocwage.t01.htm.)

9. Bureau of Labor Statistics, U.S. Department of Labor. 2005a.

10. Bureau of Labor Statistics, U.S. Department of Labor. 2005a.

11. U.S. Census Bureau 2005.

12. U.S. Census Bureau 2004.

13. Patterson 2004a:14.

14. Patterson 2003.

15. Patterson 2004b. You can read more about this online through his "Where Have All the Voters Gone?" series on the History News Network at http://hnn.us/articles/1104.html.

16. Bureau of Labor Statistics 2006.

17. Although, as Ruy Teixeira and Joel Rogers point out in *Why the White Working Class Still Matters,* the working class comprises more than half of all potential voters and can swing elections (as they seem to have done in the Presidential election of 2004), they have not been able to pressure elected officials to make their class-based issues a priority while in office.

18. Center for Responsive Politics 2005.

19. Actually, we have no one unified electoral system. Elections are handled at the county and state level, with rules for registering voters, designing ballots, type of voting machine, etc. determined by local officials rather than by the federal government.

20. Skocpol 2003.

21. Korgen and Lune Forthcoming.

22. Anyone who knows anything about the tremendous need for affordable housing in NYC (and across the nation) will particularly appreciate this story.

23. Undertaken by Jeffry Korgen for his book *My Lord and My God. . .* Mahwah, NJ: Paulist Press 2006.

24. http://www.industrialareasfoundation.org 2004.

25. *Footnotes* 2003.

26. This act was a compromise that led to allowing those applying for driver's licenses to register. Poor people applying for government aid programs were also supposed to be encouraged to register. Unfortunately, although many, many Americans register to vote while acquiring their driver's license, relatively few government officials have followed through with the Act's requirement that they register poor people.

27. Piven 2005.

❖ REFERENCES

Bucks, Brian K., Arthur B. Kennickell, and Kevin B. Moore (with Gerhard Fries and A. Michael Neal). 2006. "Recent Changes in U.S. Family Finances: Evidence from the 2001 and 2004 Survey of Consumer Finances." Federal Reserve Board Web site accessed at http://www.federalreserve.gov/pubs/bulletin/2006/financesurvey.pdf on March 15, 2006.

Bureau of Labor Statistics, U.S. Department of Labor. 2004. "Occupational Employment Statistics survey by occupation, November 2004." Accessed at http://www.bls.gov/news .release/ocwage.t01.htm on December 9, 2005.

Bureau of Labor Statistics, U.S. Department of Labor. 2005a. "A Profile of the Working Poor, 2003." Accessed at http://www.bls.gov/cps/cpswp2003 .pdf on December 4, 2005.

Bureau of Labor Statistics, U.S. Department of Labor. 2005b. "Union Members Summary." Accessed at http://www.bls.gov/news.release/union2.nr0 .htm on December 5, 2005.

Bureau of Labor Statistics, U.S. Department of Labor. 2006. "Union Members in 2005." Accessed at http://www.bls.gov/news.release/union2.t02.htm on March 15, 2006.

Center for Responsive Politics. 2005. "2004 Election Overview: Stats at a Glance." Accessed at http://www.crp.org/overview/stats.asp?cycle= 2004&type= A&display=A on December 4, 2005.

Domhoff, G. William. 1967. *Who Rules America?* 1st ed. Englewood Cliffs, NJ: Prentice Hall.

Domhoff, G. W. 1983. *Who Rules America Now?* New York: Simon and Schuster.

Domhoff, G. W. 2002. *Who Rules America?* 4th ed. New York: McGraw-Hill.

Domhoff, G. W. 2005. *Who Rules America? Power, Politics, & Social Change* 5th ed. New York: McGraw-Hill.

Footnotes. 2003. "ASA Award Recipients Honored in Atlanta." September/ October. Accessed at http://www.asanet.org/footnotes/septoct03/ fn4.html on December 5, 2005.

Johnston, David Cay. 2005. "Richest Are Leaving Even the Rich Far Behind." *The New York Times,* June 5. Accessed at http://www.nytimes.com/2005/ 06/05/national/class/HYPER-FINAL.html on June 5, 2005.

Korgen, Kathleen Odell and Howard Lune. Forthcoming. *How Sociology Can Save Democracy.* Saddle River, NJ: Prentice Hall.

Korgen, Jeffry. 2006. *My Lord and My God. . .* Mahwah, NJ: Paulist Press.

Mills, C. Wright. [1970] 1956. *The Power Elite.* New York: Oxford University Press.

Patterson, Thomas E. 2003. *The Vanishing Voter: Public Involvement in an Age of Uncertainty.* New York: Vintage.

Patterson, Thomas E. 2004a. "Where Did All the Voters Go?" *Phi Kappa Phi Forum 84*(1), Winter:11–14.

Patterson, Thomas E. 2004b. "Where Have All the Voters Gone?" Series on the History News Network at http://hnn.us/articles/1104.html on May 2, 2006.

Piven, Frances Fox. 2005. "Voting and Voters." *Logos,* Winter. Accessed at http://www.logosjournal.com/issue_4.1/piven.htm on December 5, 2005.

Skocpol, Theda. 2003. *Diminished Democracy: From Membership to Management in American Civic Life.* Norman: University of Oklahoma Press.

Teixeira, Ruy and Joel Rogers. 2000. *Why the White Working Class Still Matters.* New York: Basic Books.

U.S. Census Bureau. 2004. "Income Stable, Poverty Up, Numbers of Americans With and Without Health Insurance Rise, Census Bureau Reports." *U.S. Census Bureau News,* August 26. Accessed at http://www.census.gov/Press-Release/www/releases/ archives/income_wealth/002484.html on December 5, 2005.

U.S. Census Bureau. 2005. "Table POV1: Age and Sex of All People, Family Members and Unrelated Individuals Iterated by Income-to-Poverty Ratio and Race." Accessed at http://pubdb3.census.gov/macro/032005/pov/new01_100.htm on December 5, 2005.

Weber, Max. 1968. *Economy and Society.* Totowa, NJ: Bedminster Press.

10

Sex, Gender, and Power

I magine you have just found out that you are going to be a parent. What are your hopes and dreams for your child? What games will you play with your little one? Can you picture yourself being the coach of one of your child's sports teams? Can you imagine you and your child baking cookies together? Now, think about some of your child's characteristics. Is your child going to be tough? Sensitive? A leader? A follower?

More than likely, these questions are difficult for you to answer without first picturing whether your child will be a boy or a girl. Although the physical characteristics and genetic makeup of girls and boys play a major role in the adults they will become, so do the gender roles assigned to them. All parents see their children through glasses tinted by gender socialization. Through gender socialization, we learn to apply dissimilar social roles to boys and girls. The result is that we treat boys and girls differently and they, in turn, learn to act in "masculine" or "feminine" ways. In this chapter, we examine how gender is socially constructed, how gender construction relates to the distribution of power in society, the status of women as a minority group in the United States (minority and majority status is based on power), and how we might address the inequality of power between men and women.

❖ THE SOCIAL CONSTRUCTION OF GENDER

Whereas sex is determined by the physical characteristics that distinguish males and females,[1] gender is determined by the social roles assigned to males and females in society. As such, gender is socially constructed. Whereas sex differences remain constant (almost always[2]), gender differs over time and from society to society. For example, in the mid-1900's, there were more male than female doctors in the United States, but women dominated the medical field in the Soviet Union. Today, voting and driving are both perceived as inappropriate (and, in fact, illegal) behaviors for women in Saudi Arabia, whereas they seem natural and appropriate for women in much of the rest of the world. Here in the United States, it was historically considered inappropriate for girls to play ice hockey, both because it was thought to be too physical a game for them and because it was considered unfeminine. Over the past 15 years, as women's roles and the idea of femininity have been reconstructed, there has been an increase of nearly 1,000% in participation of girls and women in ice hockey.[3]

Exercise 10.1a   **Gender, Relationships, and Socialization**

1. Make a list of the 10 characteristics you are most looking for in a boyfriend or girlfriend.

2. On a separate piece of paper, make a list of the 10 characteristics that you think a man or woman is most looking for in you.

3. Have your professor collect these and tally up the results, following the instructions we have provided on our Web site.

4. Analyze the results. What are men most looking for? What are women most looking for? What are the differences between these? What are the causes of these differences? What are the social effects of these differences (How do they affect the gender roles and the social power of men and women)?

5. Further Analysis. What did women *think* that potential partners were looking for in them? What did men *think* that potential partners were looking for in them? Compare these results to those found in question 4. Were women or men more accurate in guessing what their potential partners were looking for? Why? How does gender socialization help to explain this? How does gender socialization promote heterosexuality at the expense of other sexual orientations?

Exercise 10.1b   **Gender Differences in Personal Advertisements**

1. Write an advertisement for the "Personals" section of a hypothetical newspaper. In your advertisement, describe yourself (at least 40 words) and what you are looking for in a partner (at least 40 words).

2. Get in groups of 4 (preferably 2 women and 2 men) and read your advertisements to each other. What do these advertisements tell you about gender?

Although people's personalities, talents, and outlooks on life are based on a combination of genetic (nature) and social (nurture) factors, sociologists focus on the social factors. In the case of gender and sexuality, we study the social roles applied to men and women through gender socialization. The process of gender socialization begins from the moment parents learn the sex of their child. Even in utero, parents treat children differently on the basis of their sex. For example, mothers who speak to their unborn children tend to do so more sharply and forcefully when they know the baby is a boy.[4] Choices of baby shower gifts and the color of the baby's room and clothes are all often based on the gender roles we assign to males and females. Even how we hold, handle, and care for babies varies according to the assigned gender roles. Although it is often impossible for strangers to tell the sex of babies if they have a diaper on, those who are perceived to be girls are treated much more gently than those who are perceived to be boys.[5]

Exercise 10.2   **A (Gendered) Tour Through a Toy Store**

Go to a major (chain) toy store and try to find a toy (not a piece of sports equipment) that could be given to either a boy or a girl. Be sure to take note of the following:

1. What is the layout of the store? Are there distinct boy and girl sections?

2. What types of toys are marketed toward girls? What types of toys are marketed toward boys?

3. What types of words and descriptions are used on the toys to market toward girls or boys?

(Continued)

(Continued)
---

4. Are there many toys that do not indicate on the packaging (e.g., have pictures of either all girls or all boys on it) the sex of the child for which they are deemed appropriate?

5. How did you find the toy you selected? Was it easy or difficult to find? Where was it located?

Based upon your experience in the toy store, write a 2–3 page paper that analyzes how toys are a means of gender socialization. What values do they teach boys and girls? For what social roles are these toys teaching and training boys and girls?

Sometimes gender socialization can have life and death consequences for babies. For example, in some Asian nations, more boy than girl babies are carried to term and born. As James Mahon notes, the culturally based preference for sons in China and the limit on how many children couples can have have resulted in "sex-selective" abortions of girls to such an extent that there are now far more boys than girls in China.[6] A similar situation exists in India, where the number of girls per 1,000 boys under the age of six dropped from 945 in 1991 to 927 in 2001.[7]

As males and females move from birth to childhood to adulthood, they learn that they are expected to conform to the gender roles society has assigned to them. This process involves learning what toys to play with, how to speak (what tone, how often, to whom, etc.), how to present oneself in public, what sports to play, what jobs or professions to consider, and so on. It also includes learning sex roles (how to act in dating situations and sexually). As they grow older, boys and girls learn different lessons about with whom it is appropriate for them to act sexually, when it is permissible to have sex, and how they should have sexual relations. Although some societies are more open than others, the majority of people in almost all modern societies view heterosexual behavior (sex between men and women) as more appropriate and socially desirable than homosexual or bisexual sexual relations. This, of course, has negative ramifications for those who, despite gender socialization, feel sexual attraction for certain people of the same sex or are sexually attracted to members of both sexes.

In general, gender roles confine members of both sexes to certain types of behavior and limit their freedom to act without fear of social disapproval. Those who vary from their gender-based roles face negative sanctions. For example, husbands who wish to stay at home and take care of their children while their wives work are often looked upon as not "true" men. The neighbor of one of the authors has been called a "girly-man" because he is taking time off from full-time employment to be at home with his young children while his wife works.[8] However, his wife faced no such negative sanctions when she stayed home with their children for the preceding three years!

All in all, though, despite the negative ramifications men face when they do not conform to their gender-based roles, the behaviors we assign to masculine and feminine roles still provide men with more social, political, and economic power than women. Although the norms for gender (and sexual[9]) roles are constantly evolving, in general, boys are trained to be tough, competitive, and self promoting,[10] whereas girls are socialized to be sensitive, cooperative, caring, and self-deprecating. These respective gender roles clearly give men an advantage in both the private and public arenas.[11]

Even in societies where there is *de jure* (legal) equality for women, gender socialization can promote *de facto* (in fact) inequality between the sexes. For example, in the United States, there are more women than men. However, women have less power than men and are, therefore, considered by sociologists and others who study power to be a minority group. Below, we outline the social, political, and economic inequalities between men and women in the United States. As you will see, these different aspects of power relations are interrelated, and feed off one another.

❖ SOCIAL INEQUALITIES

Through gender socialization, both sexes are more likely to view men than women as experts and in possession of the tools of legitimate power. The different ways men and women communicate, with men more likely to interrupt and speak over others, influences power dynamics between the sexes.[12] Men also tend to be seen as more competent, which reinforces the notion that men have more leadership abilities and should be paid attention to more than women.[13] This disparity can often be seen when men and women enter a public event, meeting, or place of business together. Almost invariably, the man will be greeted and attended to first.

The tasks that men and women are socialized to do in private households also benefit men over women. As the number of dual income households—households with couples who both hold full-time jobs—has increased, women are still expected to come home from work and to shoulder the majority of the burden for domestic chores, including cooking, cleaning, and especially child care. Arlie Hochschild has famously called this social phenomenon "the second shift."[14]

The effect of money on power in relationships is influenced by gender socialization and not evenly distributed between men and women. Family financial decisions are largely controlled by men when men earn more money than their female partners. Men also tend to have higher amounts of personal spending money than women in the same household, whereas women are more likely to deprive themselves when family finances are limited.[15] Though the power of women increases as their income rises, even wives who earn more than their partners "feel hesitant to pull the purse strings"[16] and violate the gender roles in which men are the heads of the household. This hesitancy to make use of financial power at home is consistent with gendered roles that women assume elsewhere, including in the political realm.

❖ POLITICAL INEQUALITIES

Although the First Wave of the Women's Movement led to passage of the 19th Amendment and gave women the right to vote in 1920, women are still far from attaining equal representation in politics. Today, more women vote than men. However, in 2005, women comprised only 8 out of 50 State Governors, 67 out of 425 Representatives and 14 out of 100 Senators in the U.S. Congress.[17] Globally, only 10 out of 180 current heads of state or government are female. The United States has not yet elected a female President or even a female Vice President.[18]

However, women have achieved greater political gains lower down the political ladder. For example, in 2005, 22.6% of state legislators were women, representing, according to the Center for American Women and Politics, a "four-fold" increase since 1971.[19] Although the gains in the percentage of female state legislators has slowed in recent years, the increase in female representation that has occurred at the local and state level is very important, because many officials in higher office start their political careers in these types of political positions. Still, women remain disproportionately underrepresented even on the local levels, considering that women currently comprise 51% of the total U.S. population.[20]

There is much evidence that women today, as a group, have different political opinions than men. There has been a gender gap in every

Presidential election since 1980. The gender gap refers to the difference in the percentage of women and men voting for the winning candidate. On average, since 1980, the gap has been 7.7 percentage points. For example, in 2004 55% of men but only 48% of women voted to reelect George W. Bush to the office of U.S. President.[21]

However, women, as well as men, are influenced by gender socialization. Women who run for political office (or any position of power) must, in some ways, resocialize themselves. They have to learn to be self-promoters rather than self-deprecators, to be tough rather than sensitive, and to speak up rather than defer to others. At the same time, they must trust that voters will be more impressed with their leadership credentials than turned off by their stepping out of the traditional "feminine" gender role.

Exercise 10.3   Gender, Politics, and Political Power

Go to the Web site for The White House Project at http://www.thewhite houseproject.org/index.html and click on "research and reports." Open the first link under "The White House Project Research" and the first link under "Reports." By doing, so you will find recent research about women and politics on the Web site. Read the reports found under these two links.

1. What did you learn about women and the political realm? Does the information you've uncovered surprise you at all? Why or why not?

2. Have you ever thought about running for political office? Why or why not?

3. If you have thought of running, do you think your gender would affect the likelihood of your attaining the political office you sought? Based on information found on The White House Project Web site, discuss how you think your gender would (a) affect how you would be portrayed by the media, (b) how the public would perceive you, and (c) your chances of winning.

4. If you haven't thought of running, do you think your gender has affected this decision? Why or why not? Pretend now that you are interested in running and now answer the questions posed in question 3 above.

5. Imagine you are the campaign manager for a female candidate running for President. How would you advise her? What should she

(Continued)

(Continued)

stress in her campaign speeches? How should she speak? How should she dress? What issues would you suggest she take on and what issues would you advise her to stay away from?

6. How might your advice be different if the candidate were a man? What concerns might you have that you wouldn't have if the candidate were a woman? What might you *not* have to worry about if the candidate were a man, instead of a woman?

7. What do your answers to 4 tell you about the importance of gender roles in the public imagination? What does it tell you about the social construction of these roles? What does it tell you about the connections between gender and power?

Exercise 10.4   Leadership Qualities

This exercise will require three short surveys to be administered, in sequence, to three different pools of respondents. (The easiest thing to do would be to administer the survey to three of your classes, making sure no student responds to more than one of the surveys.)

1. Create a short form with one question and space for about 10 answers. Ask the respondents to write down their sex on the top of the page. The question is "What personal qualities make one a natural leader?" Collect answers from a class that has at least 20 students.

2. Compile a list of all of the short answers (one to three words each; don't use full sentences). Then order them from the most commonly offered responses to the least common. Finally, select the top ten responses.

3. Create a form in four columns, listing the ten top personal qualities first, with check boxes in the others, using the following headings:

Personal Attributes	Masculine	Feminine	Equally Masc. & Fem.
Attribute 1			
Attribute 2			

4. Ask members of a different class (with at least 20 students) to rate each attribute as fitting best into one of the three categories. Ask the respondents to write down their sex on the top of the page.

5. Summarize how many of the popular leadership qualities are associated with masculine identity and how many are associated with feminine identity.

6. Survey a different class (with at least 20 students) using a new form listing all of the attributes that asks respondents to indicate their sex and to evaluate each attribute on a scale from least to most *desirable*, as follows:

For each of the following personal characteristics, please indicate whether you find the attribute desirable or undesirable as a feature of a woman's personality:

Personal Attributes	Most Undesirable	Neutral	Most Desirable
Attribute 1	1 2 3 4	5 6	7 8 9 10
Attribute 2	1 2 3 4	5 6	7 8 9 10

7. Average the ratings. Overall, how desirable are leadership qualities in women?

8. Modify the form in step 6 to measure how desirable those characteristics are in men. Compare results.

9. Compare the responses of male and female respondents, and write a 4–5 page paper summarizing and sociologically analyzing your results. What are the causes and effects of the trends you have identified in your data?

❖ ECONOMIC INEQUALITIES

Women have made tremendous progress in the economic sphere over the past five decades. The Civil Rights Movement and the Second Wave of the Women's Movement brought about passage of the Equal Pay Act in 1963, the Civil Rights Act in 1964, Title IX's prohibition of sex discrimination in schools (and in funding for school sports), acknowledgement of sexual harassment as a social issue, and the inclusion of women in Affirmative Action programs. These legislative acts, inflation, and the decline in the number of jobs whereby one earner could support a family contributed to the percentage of full-time female workers jumping from 41% in 1971 to 60.6% in 2006 (compared to 75.9% of men in 2006).[22]

However, significantly more women than men live in poverty. Women who are heads of households, and their children, are particularly likely to reside in poverty. In 2003, 26.5% of female-headed households lived in poverty.[23] Despite all of the above legislation and progress that the women's rights movement has made, women today still make only 77 cents for every dollar made by men[24] and still face a "glass ceiling" when trying to advance into higher levels of management for a variety of reasons, including the following:

- Gender socialization influences (a) what subjects girls study and are encouraged to study in school (e.g., girls are heavily underrepresented in math and science majors in college), (b) what career paths they are directed toward and choose, and (c) their ability to think of themselves, present themselves, and be perceived by others as capable professionals and leaders.
- Only women can become pregnant and give birth to children. If women want to have children, they must take at least some time off from work to give birth, recover from childbirth, and care for their newborn. (Paid care for newborns is very difficult to find, unless you are one of the few who can afford to hire a nanny, and it is hard to find anyone willing (even for pay) to wake up 3 times a night to change and feed your newborn).
- Women have to do the majority of child care and housework even when working, as Arlie Hochschild points out in her book *The Second Shift*. This impacts their ability to spend extra hours at their paid job and advance in their career. Ironically, this factor further fuels the stereotype that women are less capable than men and are less hardworking, when, in fact, they are juggling more and working longer hours than men (when house/child care and professional work are combined).
- Sex discrimination and sexual harassment still exist and work to hamper the economic progress of women. For example, in 2004, among the myriad sex discrimination and sexual harassment cases it handled, the Equal Employment Opportunity Commission (EEOC) forced Morgan Stanley to pay 54 million dollars to compensate for sex discrimination against female

workers; the Dial Corporation to provide 10 million dollars in damages to 90 female workers who suffered sexual harassment at the company's Montgomery, Illinois, production facility; and Federal Express to pay $3,241,400 to a female driver who experienced both sex discrimination and sexual harassment on the job.[25]

Clearly, challenges still exist for women in the social, political, and economic spheres. However, progress toward equality has been made through effective, organized efforts. Our culture and gender roles are continually changing and adjusting to the social and structural forces at work in our society. Legislation like the 19th Amendment, the Equal Pay Act of 1963, and the Civil Rights laws of 1964 that prohibited employment discrimination on the basis of sex (as well as race, color, religion, and national origin) did much to change the actions and beliefs of Americans. Sociological tools have been and will continue to be effective means for uncovering and addressing gender inequality in society. The Sociologist in Action section below, highlighting the work of Mary Gatta, is a good example of how sociology can be effectively used in this endeavor.

Sociologist in Action: Mary Gatta

Gender, race, class, age, and educational levels, among other variables, alter the effectiveness of public policies. Yet public officials and policymakers are not often trained to unpack the effects of such variables. Dr. Mary Gatta, Director of Workforce Policy and Research, at the Center for Women and Work, Rutgers University, works collaboratively with policy officials to help craft social policy and programs that take into account the effects of these variables on marginalized groups. Specifically, Gatta works with policy officials to develop and implement workforce development programs that provide access to education and skills training to single working poor mothers in ways that attend to their work and family needs. She is helping to craft programs that are flexible so that women can receive their education without comprising their family or work responsibilities.

Using a sociological framework, Gatta examines how workforce development policies are formulated and implemented in order to understand why so many such policies have not succeeded in helping poor working

(Continued)

(Continued)

women. Using her sociological eye, Gatta can see that working poor women are caught in a system in which they are not only unable to support themselves but also unable to acquire human capital resources to attain self-sufficiency via the traditional mechanisms of education and skills training. She understands that this is the double-edged sword that working poor women face: How do they economically survive day by day and then how do they attain the skills that will enable them to be more marketable for the future? Women, and in particular single working poor mothers, face a system of structural barriers—child care, elder care, irregular work hours, transportation inequities—that makes it hard for them to gain education in traditional classroom settings.

To address these issues, Gatta is overseeing a new and rapidly expanding system of training single, working mothers via the Internet. Her work enables single mothers to obtain better jobs and become more active participants in U.S. society by providing them with flexible educational alternatives. The Internet is available around the clock, so women can fit education into their lives, as opposed to fitting their lives into educational structures. In addition, these programs provide computers for the women and their children, helping to bridge the digital divide.

Gatta's background in sociology helps her to educate policymakers on gendered effects of policy. Her new book *Not Just Getting By: The New Era of Flexible Workforce Development,* which she wrote in collaboration with Kevin McCabe, a former Commissioner of Labor for New Jersey, is an excellent example of her ability to use sociology for the public good. Gatta's use of her sociological training in her work with policymakers helps them to do their job more effectively and ensures that gender is taken into account at the policy table.

Exercise 10.5   Promoting Gender Equality in the World

"Strong evidence from around the world confirms that gender equality accelerates overall economic growth, strengthens democratic governance, and reduces poverty and insecurity." Kemal Dervis, United Nations Development Programme Administrator, September 6, 2005[26]

Go to:

1. The United Nations Development Programme's (UNDP) Women's Empowerment Web site at http://www.undp.org/women/

2. The United Nations Development Fund for Women (UNIFEM) Web site at http://www.unifem.org/

3. Oxfam America's Web site at http://www.oxfamamerica.org/ (under the search link put in the word "women")

Write a four-page paper that:

1. Explains how "gender equality accelerates overall economic growth, strengthens democratic governance, and reduces poverty and insecurity"

2. Gives two examples of UN or Oxfam America programs that are promoting gender equality

3. Discusses how the success or failure of such efforts will affect women all across the globe (as members of the same minority group)

Extra Credit: Write a 1–2 page paper that uses your sociological imagination in developing the plan for a program that would promote gender equality worldwide (or in a specific country). Be creative, strategic, and specific.

❖ DISCUSSION QUESTIONS

1. Think about the division of labor along gender lines in the household in which you grew up. Who did what? Why was it like that? Would you want to repeat it in your own adult household? Why or why not? If you are married or cohabitating now, discuss how you divide the labor in your current household, and if it is similar to the way household chores were distributed in your family of origin (and why or why not).

2. What does "Equal Rights" mean to you? How much equality is there between men and women in this society?

3. Gender-role socialization begins at birth, or before. Friends and relatives want to know the sex of the expected child so that they can purchase gender-appropriate blankets, pillows, bibs, and clothes (blue or pink). The socialization continues and becomes more intense as we get older. Is it possible to raise boys and girls the same way? What are some of the obvious ways in which children are taught gender roles? Can we change those? Should we? If so, how? Be specific in outlining some proactive ways to change gender roles and expectations.

4. How are gender roles related to sex roles? What do they teach us about how to act sexually and with whom to have sex?

5. Why should women in the United States care about the status of women in Bangladesh or Ethiopia or some other seemingly faraway nation? Is there any responsibility for the U.S. women's movement to participate in the global women's movement? Why or why not? If so, what are some of the ways that U.S. women can contribute?

6. Why should men be interested in promoting equality for women?

7. Would you feel (a) more comfortable and (b) more secure with a female or male President? Why? How do you think gender socialization influenced your answer? How do you think classes that made you aware of gender socialization influenced your answer? If you answered that you would feel more secure with a man as President, what would need to happen to change your mind?

8. What do you think would be the most effective way to diminish social inequality between the sexes in the United States? What do you think would be the most effective way to diminish political inequality between the sexes in the United States? What do you think would be the most effective way to diminish economic inequality between the sexes in the United States?

❖ SUGGESTIONS FOR SPECIFIC ACTIONS

1. Interested in promoting economic equality for women? Go to the 9 to 5 organization's Web site at http://www.9to5.org/ and go to the "Take Action" link. Read about the efforts 9 to 5 is taking to fight for the issues of working women. If you want to become part of one of the 9 to 5 campaigns, follow the steps on their "take action" page.

2. Help women's collectives in a developing country by supporting an alternative income program that will allow them to gain economic and social power in their societies. Learn about the collectives by going to http://www.freethechildren.com/programs/alternativeincome/alternativeincome_women.htm.

Then, go to http://www.aidmatrix.org/adoptavillage/ and help raise the money to Adopt a Village!

3. Read about the Women's Rights Protocol from Human Rights Watch at https://hrw.org/women/africaprotocol/ and then take the actions they suggest (letter writing, etc.) to urge African governments to ratify this important legislation.

Please go to our Web site at http://www.sagepub.com/korgen to find further civic engagement opportunities, resources, and peer-reviewed articles related to this chapter.

❖ ENDNOTES

1. A very small percentage of the population is born with both male and female sexual characteristics. Almost always, an operation is performed shortly after birth to make the child's sex organs primarily male or female (usually female).

2. Sex change operations, although very painful and expensive, are possible. However, few people want to go through them and even fewer have the opportunity to have such operations.

3. See http://www.whockey.com/country/usa/.

4. Smith 2005.

5. MacDonald and Parke 1986.

6. Mahon 2005.

7. Mudur 2002.

8. His comments about making conversations with the other parents (all mothers!) waiting to pick up their children from school are quite amusing. While he can hold his own in the conversations about laundry, he'd much rather be discussing football. Just because people have the power to defy some gender role expectations does not mean that gender socialization has not affected them at all.

9. For example, same sex marriage is now legal in Massachusetts (and in nearby Canada).

10. And taught to distance themselves from "girlish" behavior. The saying "you throw like a girl" is one of the many ways boys are taught to be anything but "like a girl."

11. Commuri and Gentry 2005.

12. Tannen 2001.

13. Carli 1999.

14. Hochschild 2003.

15. Commuri et al. 2005.

16. Pahl 2000.

17. See the Center for American Women and Politics (CAWP) at http://www.cawp.rutgers.edu/index.html for more information about women in the political realm.

18. Yahoo. "Women World Leaders." 2005.

19. CAWP 2005.

20. Spraggins, Renee E. 2005. *We the People: Women and Men in the United States.* Accessed at www.census.gov/prod/2005pubs/censr-20.pdf on January 11, 2006.

21. Walsh 2005.

22. Bureau of Labor Statistics, United States Department of Labor 2005 and 2006.

23. Proctor and Dalaker 2003.

24. U.S. Census Bureau 2005.

25. The U.S. Equal Opportunity Employment Commission 2004.

26. The Dervis quote is found on the United Nations Development Programme Web site at http://www.undp.org/gender/.

❖ REFERENCES

Bureau of Labor Statistics, U.S. Department of Labor. 2005. "Women in the Labor Force: A Databook Updated and Available on the Internet." May 13. Accessed at http://www.bls.gov/bls/databooknews2005.pdf on January 10, 2005.

Bureau of Labor Statistics, U.S. Department of Labor. 2006. "Table A-1: Employment Status of the Civilian Population by Sex and Age." Accessed at http://www.bls.gov/news.release/empsit.t01.htm on March 15, 2006.

Carli, Linda L. 1999. "Gender, Interpersonal Power, and Social Influence." *Journal of Social Issues* 55, Spring: 81–100.

Center for American Women and Politics (CAWP). Accessed at http://www.cawp.rutgers.edu/index.html on May 3, 2006.

CAWP. 2005. "Women in Elective Office 2005." Accessed at http://www.cawp.rutgers.edu/Facts/Officeholders/cawpfs.html on January 9, 2006.

Commuri, Suraj and James W. Gentry. 2005. "Resource Allocation in Households with Women as Chief Wage Earners." *Journal of Consumer Research* 32, September: 185–95.

Gatta, Mary, with Kevin McCabe. 2005. *Not Just Getting By: The New Era of Flexible Workforce Development.* Lanham, MD: Lexington Books.

Hochschild, Arlie Russell, with Anne Machung. 2003. *The Second Shift.* New York: Penguin Books.

MacDonald, Kevin and Ross D. Parke. 1986. "'Parental—Child' Physical Play: The Effects of Sex and Age of Children and Parents." *Sex Roles* 15: 367–78.

Mahon, James. 2005. "Weber's Protestant Ethic and the Chinese Preference for Sons: An Application of Western Sociology to Eastern Religion." *Max Weber Studies* 5(1): 59–80.

Mudur, Ganapati. 2002. "India plans new legislation to prevent sex selection." *British Medical Journal 324*(7334): 385.

Pahl, Jan. 2000. "Couples and Their Money: Patterns of Accounting and Accountability in the Domestic Economy." *Accounting, Auditing & Accountability Journal 13*(4): 502–17.

Proctor, Bernadette D. and Joseph Dalaker. 2003. "U.S. Census Bureau. Current Population Reports. P60-222," *Poverty in the United States, 2002.* Washington, DC: U.S. Government Printing Office.

Smith, Kara. 2005. "Prebirth Gender Talk: A Case Study in Prenatal Socialization." *Women & Language 28*(1), Spring: 49–53.

Tannen, Deborah. 2001. *You Just Don't Understand: Women and Men in Conversation.* New York: HarperCollins.

U.S. Census Bureau. 2005. "Income Stable, Poverty Rate Increases, Percentage of Americans Without Health Insurance Unchanged." *U.S. Census Bureau News,* August 30. Accessed at http://www.census.gov/Press-Release/www/releases/archives/income_wealth/005647.html on January 10, 2006.

The U.S. Equal Opportunity Employment Commission. 2004. "Office of General Counsel FY 2004 Annual Report—Summary of Accomplishments." Accessed at http://www.eeoc.gov/litigation/04annrpt/index.html#IID1 on January 10, 2006.

Walsh, Debbie. 2005. "Voters for 85 Years, Women Make a Difference." CAWP Press release, August 23. Accessed at http://www.cawp.rutgers.edu/News/CAWPpress-womenvoting.pdf on January 9, 2006.

Yahoo. 2005. "Women World Leaders." Accessed at http://www.geocities.com/CapitolHill/Lobby/4642/#section1 on January 10, 2006.

11

What Does a "Typical American" Look Like Today?

Race and Ethnicity

D oes race matter? How you answer that question has a lot to do with your own experiences and your knowledge about society. Your answer also depends on your understanding of how racial groups have been treated throughout the history of the United States. In this chapter, we will examine the relationship between immigration and race–ethnicity,[1] the social construction of race, and the persistence of racism in the "colorblind" era.

❖ IMMIGRATION AND RACE–ETHNICITY

Emblazoned on the Statue of Liberty is a poem representing the Statue as the "mother of exiles" as it proclaims "worldwide welcome" to those spurned by other nations. The "mother of exiles" tells the other nations to

Give me your tired, your poor,
Your huddled masses yearning to breathe free,
The wretched refuse of your teeming shore.
Send these, the homeless, tempest-tost to me.[2]

Ironically, this poem was written a year after the enactment of the first law to restrict immigration in the United States, the Chinese Exclusion Act of 1882.

Whereas earlier immigrants came primarily from northern and western Europe, the late 1800s saw southern and eastern Europeans seeking economic opportunity or refuge from persecution. On the west coast, Chinese and Japanese immigrants also began to arrive, looking for jobs. Pseudoscience that "proved" western Europeans were from a race superior to eastern Europeans, southern Europeans, and all people of color spurred racial prejudice (negative feelings) and discrimination (harmful actions) against the groups deemed to be inferior. This racism, coupled with periodic economic downturns that led to increased competition for work, led to restricted race-based immigration policies that remained in place until 1965.

After the Chinese Exclusion Act and the Gentlemen's Agreement of 1907, which largely curtailed Japanese immigration, a series of further laws prohibited or limited immigration among non-Western Europeans. These restrictions on immigration culminated in the National Origins Acts of 1921 and 1924, which established quotas and allowed only a trickle of immigration to continue. The 1924 Immigration Act enacted 2% immigration quotas per nation, based on the 1890[3] U.S. Census. So, for example, Italy could send only 2% of the number of Italian people residing in the United States in 1890. A provision to the 1924 Act limited immigration to those eligible for citizenship. Because only those of White and African American descent could become citizens, this, in effect, prohibited all further Asian immigration.

These restrictions remained in effect until the Immigration Act of 1965 was passed at the height of the Civil Rights movement and amidst worldwide pressure to overturn legalized racial discrimination in the United States. It abolished national quotas (replacing them with quotas for the Eastern and Western Hemispheres) and did much to increase immigration and alter the racial makeup of the United States. The foreign-born population rose from 4.7% in 1970[4] to 11.7% in 2003.[5] Among those U.S. residents who were born outside the United States in 2003, 53.3% were from Latin America, 25.0% were from Asia, 13.7% were from Europe, and 8% were from other areas of the globe.

Exercise 11.1   Africa and the Legacy of Colonialism

At the same time the Civil Rights Movement was underway in the United States, a global movement for Black rights was taking place. One of the results of this global movement was the end of colonial rule in Africa (all of Africa, except Liberia and Ethiopia, was colonized by European nations).

1. Go to the Library of Congress' Country Studies Web site at http://rs6 .loc.gov/frd/cs/cshome.html.

2. Select an African nation (aside from Liberia and Ethiopia) and write a background paper that includes information about (a) when it was colonized, (b) what nation colonized it, (c) when it became a free nation, (d) how its borders were established, (e) how the establishment of its borders affects the nation today, and (f) the overall legacy of colonialism on the nation.

As you will recall from earlier chapters, the process of globalization has benefited some nations at the expense of others. Latin American nations, in particular, have suffered under globalization. The status of various immigrant groups reflects the global status of their nation of origin and their levels of education. Most Latin American nations are extremely poor, with many of their citizens drawn to the United States to find work.[6] It is important to understand that people do not generally just up and leave their homes and families unless they are desperate. Some of today's immigrants are even desperate enough to cross the dangerous Mexican–U.S. border illegally[7] to find jobs in the United States.

Some Asian immigrants (such as war refugees from Vietnam, Cambodia, and Laos) came to the United States with little money or education. Today, some Asians are brought over illegally to work as indentured servants in sweatshops in the Chinatowns in major cities. The vast majority of Asians immigrating to the United States today, however, are educated people with some money, who immigrate legally to find greater economic opportunity than exists in their former nations. On the other hand, Latin American immigrants are better able to enter the United States in relatively large numbers without either education or money because of their relative proximity to the United States. One result of the disparity in education levels of the different entering immigrant groups is the positions they achieve in the U.S. workforce and in their subsequent socioeconomic status. For example, the percentage of foreign-born individuals in management and professional occupations is highest among Asians (47%) and lowest among those from Latin America (12.7%), particularly from Central America (7.9%).[8]

❖ THE SOCIAL CONSTRUCTION OF RACE

How do you know what race you are? It depends on where and when you live. Race is a social construction, meaning that it is defined differently from society to society and sometimes, over time, even within the same society. For example, unlike the United States, Brazil has gradations between White and Black within its system of racial demarcation. In the U.S. some groups have been placed in different racial categories over time. For example, in the 1930 U.S. Census, Mexican Americans were included under the category "Mexican." However, in 1940, they were placed under "White" "unless they appeared to census interviewers to be 'definitely Indian or of other Nonwhite races' (U.S. Bureau of the Census 1943:3)."[9] Today, they can choose any race but are considered to be Hispanic–Latino (the one ethnic option listed under the racial category section on the census). In many ways, Hispanics–Latinos are treated like a distinct racial group because of their appearance and language or accent (which varies and largely determines the extent to which they face racial discrimination[10]).

Many young Italian and Irish Americans may be surprised to learn that most Americans considered Irish[11] and Italian Americans to be "less than" White until decades after they arrived in the U.S. in large numbers. Today, sociologists define a race as a group of people *perceived* to be a distinct group on the basis of physical appearance (not genetic makeup[12]). Ethnicity refers to cultural, rather than physical differences. This all gets even more complicated when dealing with Hispanic–Latino Americans, who, as noted above, are a distinct ethnic umbrella group but can be of any race.

Today, the racial–ethnic makeup of the United States is still mostly White. However, the percentages of Hispanic–Latinos and Asian Americans are rapidly increasing. Table 11.1 indicates the racial demographics of the United States based on 2000 Census figures.[13]

A "biracial baby boom" over the three decades since the Supreme Court struck down laws against interracial marriage in 1967 has added to the diversity. Between 1970 and 2000, the racial intermarriage rate grew from less than 1% to 5% of all marriages. In 1970, only 0.4% of

Table 11.1   U.S. Racial Demographics

Race	Percentage
White (not Hispanic–Latino)	69.1
Hispanic–Latino	12.5
Black	12.3
Asian	3.6
American Indian or Alaskan Native	0.7

Note: Based on 2000 Census figures.

married Whites were in interracial marriages. Today, 3% of married Whites are married to someone who is non-White. Similarly, the Black interracial-marriage rate has moved from 1% to 7%. At the present time, 16% of married Asian Americans in the United States are married to a non-Asian and approximately 25% of Hispanics–Latinos marry a non-Hispanic–Latino (usually a White person).[14] In 2000, when people were allowed to choose more than one race on the U.S. Census for the first time, 2.4% of the population did so. An additional 5.5% said they were some "other" race than those listed on the Census.[15]

Some sociologists who research racial issues maintain that the racial classification system in the United States is changing. George Yancey[16] and others maintain that Asians and Hispanics–Latinos will eventually "become White." Other scholars such as Eduardo Bonilla-Silva, say that the United States is beginning to establish a three-tiered racial hierarchy with *Whites* ("'traditional' whites, new 'white' immigrants; and, in the near future, assimilated Latinos, some multiracials [light-skinned ones], and individual members of other groups [some Asian Americans, etc.]") at the top. Next will come a middle group comprised of *"honorary Whites"* (most light-skinned Latino Americans, "Japanese Americans, Korean Americans, Asian Indians, Chinese Americans, the bulk of multiracials ... and most Middle Eastern Americans"). The bottom group, the *"collective Black,"* will consist of Black Americans, dark-skinned Latino Americans, Vietnamese Americans, Cambodian Americans, Laotian Americans, and maybe Filipino Americans.[17,18]

No matter what the *future* racial hierarchy will look like, racial inequity continues to exist in the present-day United States. W.E.B. Du Bois, one of the founders of sociology and an ardent advocate for the rights of Black Americans, wrote in 1903 that "the problem of the twentieth century is the problem of the color-line."[19] Unfortunately, the color-line (albeit shifting) is still very much a problem today. Even though race is socially constructed, the consequences of racism are real.

Although Civil Rights Laws and Affirmative Action programs abolished *de jure* (by law) discrimination and provided some opportunities for well-educated minorities to rise in socioeconomic status, *de facto* (by practice) racial discrimination persists. Black and Hispanic Americans still lag behind most other racial groups of Americans in terms of income, wealth, education, and employment. According to the U.S. Census Bureau, whereas the median family income for all Americans in 2004 was $44,389, it was $30,134 for Black and $34,241 for Hispanic Americans.[20] Wealth, which requires time to accumulate, reveals even starker disparities between White and Black and Hispanic Americans. The respective wealth of both Hispanics and Blacks is only one-tenth that of Whites.[21] Whereas 25.7% of White Americans are college graduates, only 15.6% of Black and 10.3 % of Hispanic Americans have a college degree.[22] In 2006, the unemployment rate was 4.1% for White Americans, 5.5% for Hispanic–Latino Americans and 9.3% for Black Americans.[23]

Is this news to you? If you are White, it may well be. The research of many sociologists reveals that "many Whites are under the false impression that the socioeconomic playing field *is* now level."[24] This ignorance is largely due to the way race has been depicted in the mass media since the mid-1990s.

The media has a powerful effect on how Whites perceive racial minorities, particularly Black Americans,[25] because that is the only place most Whites see and "get to know" people of color. Very few Whites live in racially integrated neighborhoods. So, they tend to formulate their opinions about minority socioeconomic status (and everything else about racial minorities) from what they see in the media. Unfortunately, what the media tends to portray is that race-based disparities no longer exist. In magazines, movies, television, and so forth, U.S. society is portrayed as if race no longer matters. Interracial couples and integrated friendship groups are depicted in advertisements for everything from restaurants to sneakers; popular television shows like *Grey's Anatomy* and *Lost* have interracial casts that never speak about race; and rarely do news programs or public officials devote time to exposing and analyzing the great racial disparities that continue to persist in the United States today.

Exercise 11.2	Survey on Race in the U.S.

Conduct a survey of the members of one of your classes. On the survey, ask them

- their race
- their ethnicity
- to respond to the following statements:

    (Provide them with the following options and ask them to circle one to indicate their level of agreement with the statement: Strongly Agree, Somewhat Agree, Not Sure, Somewhat Disagree, Strongly Disagree)

    1. The socio-economic status of White and Black Americans is relatively equal.

    2. Racism is often exaggerated by members of minority groups.

    3. People of all races have relatively equal chances to become successful in the United States today.

- what, if any, college courses they have taken that deal with racial and ethnic relations

Compare the answers of respondents of (a) different racial–ethnic groups and (b) those who have and those who have not taken any courses that deal with racial and ethnic relations. Explain your results.

❖ THE COLORBLIND IDEOLOGY

A popular view among many Americans today, particularly White Americans, is that race no longer matters. They maintain that we should all act as though we are "colorblind" when it comes to race. Many even go so far as to say that people who talk about and notice racial differences are actually causing racial friction that would otherwise not exist. However, we know this is far from true. As you will remember from Chapter Seven, France provides a powerful example of how racial discrimination can exist in a nation that does not officially recognize race or keep racial statistics.

Partly in response to the influence of the colorblind ideology, most people feel uncomfortable noticing racial differences or talking about race, particularly with members of another race (those most likely to provide us with a different perspective). One of the authors found through her research[26] that even Blacks and Whites who are close friends tend to avoid talking about racial issues. This avoidance is problematic for anyone interested in promoting racial justice. If we want to end racial discrimination, we have to acknowledge that races are treated differently.

Before we can effectively fight racial discrimination, we must uncover and confront it. We must also make the "invisible privileges"[27] of Whiteness visible. To do so, we need to notice and keep track of how different racial groups are treated. For example, the U.S. Department of Housing and Urban Development could not have conducted the studies in 1989 and 2000 that revealed that "housing discrimination against Blacks and Hispanics is declining but still remains a significant national problem,"[28] if they were not allowed to group people by race. Nor would we know that today, in New York City, Whites have a greater chance than Hispanics and fully twice the likelihood of equally qualified Blacks of being hired.[29] These and many, many other studies illustrate conclusively that race *does* matter and that we cannot be colorblind when it comes to creating and implementing policy in the United States.

The colorblind perspective on race also runs counter to the discipline of sociology. The colorblind ideology does more than impact the efforts of racial justice organizations and policymakers working toward better equality of opportunity and outcome. It also undermines two of the most powerful goals of sociology: to observe how society really works and to give voice to the marginalized and minority groups within it.

Exercise 11.3   Has Dr. Martin Luther King Jr.'s Dream Been Realized?

1. Go to http://www.stanford.edu/group/King/publications/speeches/ address_at_march_on_washington.pdf.

2. Read Martin Luther King Jr.'s "I Have a Dream" speech.

3. List the points King makes about when he will be "satisfied" with the situation of Black people in America.

4. Check off those that have now been achieved. *Provide evidence* for your decisions to check off or not check off each point. Some of these may be partially achieved whereas others may have been fully achieved or not at all.

5. Overall, do you think Martin Luther King Jr. would be satisfied with the status of Black Americans today? Why or why not? If not, how do you suggest that we move toward a fuller realization of his dream? What specific policy recommendations would you make?

Exercise 11.4　White Privilege

Peggy McIntosh did much to bring White privilege to public recognition with her essay "White Privilege: Unpacking the Invisible Knapsack,"[30] in which she listed some of the "daily effects of White privilege" on her life.

- If you are White, come up with a list of approximately ten privileges that you (personally) receive for being White. (Do not, for example, state that you would have an easier time getting a mortgage unless you actually have a mortgage and you had an easy time getting it.)

- If you are a person of color, come up with a list of approximately ten privileges that you think a White person receives for being White.

- Compare your answers with those of other members of the class. What are the most significant differences among the lists? Who do you think had the most difficult time coming up with the ten privileges? Who had the easiest time? Why?

Exercise 11.5　Your Family and Issues of Race

Write a 1–2 page paper that answers the following questions:

1. When you were growing up, what did you hear about racial issues from your family? (e.g., Were racial issues ever seriously discussed? If so, why and how often was race a topic of serious discussion? Did your family tend to bring up race only when making jokes or insulting comments about members of other races? Did they speak from a viewpoint of colorblindness and thus discourage any discussion of the real, pressing issues associated with race and racism?)

2. How do you think the racial makeup of your family influenced how race was discussed (or not discussed) in your family?

3. How do your answers to the first two questions relate to what you have learned in this chapter? How does the information in this chapter help you, if at all, to reevaluate your views on race, immigration, and racism?

Sociologist in Action: George Yancey

Martin Luther King once said that Sunday morning is "the most segregated time of the week." George Yancey is committed to the day when this statement is no longer the case. He works with a half-million dollar Lilly grant and with Dr. Michael Emerson and Dr. Karen Chai to conduct the first national attempt to map out and understand multiracial churches. From the work of this grant he has written *One Body, One Spirit,* a book that is marketed toward Christians and that dispenses practical advice as to how they can racially diversify their congregations. In this way Yancey is able to translate his academic research into a written format that nonacademics can use.

In addition to writing for this audience, Yancey has also consulted with churches that are seeking to become more racially diverse. Using quantitative and qualitative methodology, he is able to assess social and cultural patterns within the churches that may unintentionally set up barriers against potential worshippers of other races. In addition to his consulting, Yancey also is working with Mosaix (www.mosaix.info), an organization which is committed to building a network of multiracial congregations. Within the framework of this emerging network, Yancey can also disseminate results of his research as well as aid others who are supportive of developing racially diverse congregations.

Racially diverse congregations will not be possible unless some of the misunderstandings and stereotypes that have developed between Christians of different races are resolved. To this end, Yancey has written to the Christian audience about dealing with racial issues. For example he and his wife Sherelyn have edited work about interracial families for Christian audiences in a book entitled *Just Don't Marry One.* His writings in such works are a mixture of sociological thought and Christian theology. Thus they are designed to reach a nonacademic group by speaking in the language of his intended audience.

❖ DISCUSSION QUESTIONS

1. Close your eyes and picture an American citizen. What does the person you pictured look like? Why do you think you imagined the race–ethnicity of the person in the way that you did? (It might be interesting to ask people who are not in this class the same question after you have answered for yourself. If you only ask them to "describe" the person, note whether they mention race.)

2. Do you have a good friend of a different race? If so, how did you meet? Do you ever talk seriously about racial issues? Why or why not? If you do not have a good friend of another race, why do you think this is?

3. How can sociology be used to (a) recognize, (b) publicize, and (c) combat racial discrimination? Be specific and clearly explain your answers.

4. Why do you think so many people want to believe that "race doesn't matter anymore"? What do you think would happen if we no longer kept track of different racial groups in our society? What might be the beneficial effects of not doing so? What might be the negative consequences?

5. What do you think your parents would say if you told them you were going to marry someone of a different race? Why? Would it depend on *what* race? Why?

6. What are some ways that racial discrimination takes place in our public school systems without anyone *intentionally* doing anything to harm a particular racial group? What are some ways unintended racial discrimination occurs on your own campus?

7. Which groups of prospective students (other than racial groups) have an easier time gaining admittance and paying for a college education than other prospective students? Why do you think people have a harder time with race-based affirmative action programs, rather than the preferential treatment given to other (non-race-based) groups?

8. Do you think multiracial Americans should be given a separate box on the U.S. Census? What do you think would be some outcomes of the establishment of such a box?

9. What is the difference between *prejudice* and *discrimination*? How can you detect prejudice if there is not evidence of discrimination?

❖ SUGGESTIONS FOR SPECIFIC ACTIONS

1. Conduct interviews with top administrators at your school to find out (a) what they think is the obligation of an institution of

higher education in combating racism in society and (b) what specific things your school is doing to combat racism in society. If you think the school should be doing more, organize a group of likeminded students, faculty, and staff to create more antiracism efforts on campus.

2. Go to the NAACP Web site at http://www.naacp.org/opera tions/member/member_volunteer.html. Look over the volunteer opportunities listed there and find one you are interested in pursuing. Find the number of your local NAACP chapters (through calling 877-NAACP-98) and offer your services. *Or* join or volunteer with another race–ethnicity based organization (e.g., MANA at http://www.hermana.org/homfrm.htm, League of United Latin American Citizens at http://www .lulac.org/, Conference on Asian Pacific American Leadership (CAPAL) at http://www.capal.org/who_we_are.html, American Indian Movement at http://www.aimovement.org/index .html).

Please go to our Web site at http://www.sagepub.com/korgen to find further civic engagement opportunities, resources, and peer-reviewed articles related to this chapter.

❖ ENDNOTES

1. Although we note below that ethnicity and race are two distinct concepts, we group them together in several places in this chapter. We typically do so when we are including Hispanics–Latinos in the discussion because Hispanics–Latinos are an *ethnic* group that tends to be viewed—both by its own members and by other Americans—as a distinct *racial* group.

2. Lazarus 1883.

3. The quotas were based on the U.S. population back in 1890, when the numbers of darker-skinned Europeans (like Italians) were lower than they were in 1924.

4. Gibson and Lennon 1999.

5. Larsen 2004.

6. Just as many poor Europeans were during the earlier periods of immigration.

7. To enter and settle in the United States legally, immigrants must either prove that they have close family members living legally in the United States (whom they would join) or that they have a certain occupational skill that is in short supply in the United States. However, the waiting list even among those eligible to receive a visa is very long because the demand to enter the United States far exceeds the quota allowed.

8. Larsen 2004.

9. Rodriguez 2000.

10. Rodriguez 2000.

11. In the middle decades of the 1800s, Irish Americans were commonly portrayed in newspaper and magazine cartoons as apes.

12. Which we now know, thanks to the Human Genome Project, varies more within than between races. Lynn B. Jorde and Stephen P. Wooding. 2004. "Genetic Variation, Classification and 'Race.'" *Nature Genetics* 36: S28–S33. Accessed at http://www.nature.com/ng/journal/v36/n11s/full/ng1435 .html on December 19, 2005.

13. U.S. Census Bureau 2001.

14. Lee and Edmonston 2005.

15. These figures do not add up to 100 because they are based on selections of race by individuals (and individuals could select more than one race in the 2000 Census).

16. Yancey 2003.

17. Bonilla-Silva and Embrick 2005.

18. Bonilla-Silva and Embrick acknowledge that some individual members of these groups may fall outside the designated tier.

19. Du Bois [1903] 1989.

20. U.S. Census Bureau 2005.

21. Kochhar 2004.

22. U.S. Census Bureau 2004.

23. Bureau of Labor Statistics 2006.

24. Gallagher 2005. For a full discussion of this, see p. 108.

25. Black Americans are more isolated than either Hispanic or Asian Americans (see Zubrinsky 2003).

26. Korgen 2002.

27. Rothenberg 2004.

28. Reade 2003.

29. Schultz and Barnes 2005.

30. McIntosh 1989.

❖ REFERENCES

Bonilla-Silva, Eduardo and David G. Embrick. 2005. "Black, Honorary White, White: The Future of Race in the United States." Pp. 33–48 in *Mixed Messages: Multiracial Identities in the Color-Blind Era,* edited by David Brunsma. Boulder: Lynne Rienner Publishers, Inc.

Bureau of Labor Statistics, U.S. Department of Labor. 2006. Employment Situation Summary, February. Accessed at http://www.bls.gov/news .release/empsit.nr0.htm on March 16, 2006.

Du Bois, W.E.B. [1903] 1989. *The Souls of Black Folk.* New York: Penguin Books.

Gallagher, Charles. 2005. "Colorblindness: An Obstacle to Racial Justice?" Pp. 103–116 in *Mixed Messages: Multiracial Identities in the Color-Blind Era*, edited by David Brunsma. Boulder: Lynne Rienner.

Gibson, Campbell J. and Emily Lennon. 1999. "Historical Census Statistics on the Foreign-Born Population of the United States: 1850 to 1990." Working Paper No. 29, U.S. Bureau of the Census, Population Division. Accessed at http://www.census.gov/population/www/documentation/twps0029/twps0029.html on December 19, 2005.

Jorde, Lynn B. and Stephen P. Wooding. 2004. "Genetic Variation, Classification and 'Race.'" *Nature Genetics* 36: S28–S33. Accessed at http://www.nature.com/ng/journal/v36/n11s/full/ng1435.html on December 19, 2005.

Kochhar, Rakesh. 2004. "The Wealth of Hispanic Households1996 to 2002." The Pew Hispanic Center Web site. Accessed at http://pewhispanic.org/reports/report.php?ReportID=34 on December 16, 2005.

Korgen, Kathleen Odell. 2002. *Crossing the Racial Divide: Close Friendships Between Black and White Americans*. Praeger Publishers: Westport, CT.

Larsen, Luke J. 2004. "The Foreign-Born Population in the United States: 2003." *Current Population Reports*. Accessed at http://www.census.gov/prod/2004pubs/p20-551.pdf on December 20, 2005.

Lazarus, Emma. [1883] 2005. "The New Colossus." Academy of American Poets accessed at http://www.poets.org/index.php on December 11, 2005.

Lee, Sharon M. and Barry Edmonston. 2005. "New Marriages, New Families: U.S. Racial and Hispanic Intermarriage." *Population Bulletin*. June. Accessed at http://www.prb.org/pdf05/60.2NewMarriages.pdf on December 19, 2005.

McIntosh, Peggy. 1989. "White Privilege: Unpacking the Invisible Knapsack." Accessed at http://www.cwru.edu/president/aaction/UnpackingThe Knapsack.pdf on May 3, 2006.

Reade, Julia. 2003. "Testing for Housing Discrimination: Findings from a HUD Study of Real Estate Agents." Accessed at http://www.bos.frb.org/commdev/c&b/2003/spring/testing.pdf on December 19, 2005.

Rodriguez, Clara E. 2000. *Changing Race: Latinos, the Census, and the History of Ethnicity in the United States*. New York: New York University Press. P. 84.

Rothenberg, Paula. 2004. *Invisible Privilege: A Memoir About Race, Class, and Gender*. Lawrence, KS: University Press of Kansas.

Schultz, Steven and Steven Barnes. 2005. "Many New York employers discriminate against minorities, ex-offenders." *News@Princeton*. April 1. Accessed at http://www.princeton.edu/main/news/archive/S11/23/70K64/index.xml?section=newsreleases on December 19, 2005.

U.S. Census Bureau. 2001. "Table 3. Population by Race Alone, Race in Combination Only, Race Alone or in Combination, and Hispanic or Latino Origin for the United States: 2000." 2000 U.S. Census. Accessed at http://www.census.gov/population/cen2000/phc-t1/tab03.pdf on December 20, 2005.

U.S. Census Bureau. 2004. "Table 2. Educational Attainment of the Population 15 Years and Over, by Single Years of Age, Sex, Race, and Hispanic Origin." Accessed at http://www.census.gov/population/www/socdemo/education/cps2004.html on March 16, 2006.

U.S. Census Bureau. 2005. "Income Stable, Poverty Rate Increases, Percentages of Americans Without Health Insurance Unchanged." Accessed at http://www.census.gov/Press-Release/www/releases/archives/income_wealth/005647.html on July 24, 2006.

Yancey, George. 2003. *Who is White? Latinos, Asians, and the New Black/NonBlack Divide*. Boulder: Lynne Rienner.

Zubrinsky, Charles Camille. 2003. "The Dynamics of Racial Residential Segregation." *Annual Review of Sociology* 29(1): 167–207.

12

The Engaged Sociologist in Action

C ongratulations! After reading this book and completing exercises
in the earlier chapters, you have no doubt developed a sociological eye and can make use of the sociological imagination. Now there's
no turning back. With a toolbox packed full with *sociological* tools, you
can not help but perceive social patterns that affect all of us but are
often unnoticed by those without your sociological training. The best
news is that you have also acquired the means to be an effective agent
of social change!

Through this sociology class (and perhaps through other means, as
well), you have developed the skills you need to become an informed
and effective citizen who can help shape our society. But, as any good
superhero knows, with great power comes responsibility. Your
sociological training allows you to understand how society works. It is
your obligation now to use that knowledge to influence society in ways
that will make it better. And just as a carpenter must not only purchase
tools but also learn how to use them properly, so must a sociologist in
action learn how to use her or his tools. So, you will practice using your
sociological tools to research and address social issues by completing
one of the projects we outline below.

The Basic Steps of Social Science Research

No matter which exercise you choose, you will need to follow the basic steps of all social science research:

1. Choose a research topic.
2. Find out what other researchers have discovered about that topic.
3. Choose a methodology (how you will collect your data).
4. Collect and analyze your data.
5. Relate your findings to those of other researchers.
6. Do something with your findings!

❖ PROJECT

Select one of the projects below.

Project 12.1 | **Civic Engagement and Higher Education**

In recent years, many educators and leaders in society have talked and written about the obligation of colleges and universities to "educate citizens."[1]

However, it is still not clear (a) how many *students* think civic engagement should be a part of a college education and (b) how many students are socially active. You will answer these questions about students on your campus and devise ways to encourage them to play an active role in shaping society.

Project 12.2 | **Social Responsibility on Campus**

Is your college or university a "socially responsible" institution? In this project you will (a) use different indicators of "social responsibility" to measure how socially responsible your school is and (b) use your findings in an effort to make your school more socially responsible.

Some of the questions to consider are: Does everyone on campus have equal access to education and other resources? Are workers paid fairly and treated fairly? Do athletes wear or does your campus store sell apparel made in sweatshops? Does your university recycle everything that it can? Is your university invested in corporations that are cited for human rights violations? Are female and male professors compensated equally? Would students know if your school were not acting in socially responsible ways?

Project 12.3   Connecting the Campus to the Community

What are the needs of the community around your college? Are they being met? Does your college or university seek out input from local leaders on how it might help the community in which it resides? Do student groups and clubs connect the student body with the local community? Is there a chasm (social or status) between the college community and the larger community? Do students have prejudices toward the local community or does the local community have prejudices toward students? Does your college contribute to the economic well-being of the greater community? This project will examine the social and economic environment of the community of which your school is a part and determine to what extent your school is working to improve the vitality of the community.

❖ STEP 1: RESEARCH PREPARATION

A. What You (Think You) Know

Before you start your research, it is important to take stock of what you *think* you know about the topics and *why* you think you know it. This will help you to focus your thinking and to make you aware of some of the potential biases you may have toward the issue. Write a one-page paper that (a) describes what you hypothesize (think) will be the answer to your research question; and (b) supports your hypothesis with examples from your own life, previous research you have done, and your "best guess" sociological analysis.

B. Reviewing the Literature

The next step is to examine previous research on your topic. Go to your school library and locate the databases of academic articles in the social sciences. We recommend Sociological Abstracts or JSTOR (indexes used to find sociological journal articles), although you can use others so long as you are searching sociology journals only. Conduct several searches for articles using any combination of keywords or phrases such as

For project 12.1 "student activism," "student apathy," "college and activism," "civic engagement and college," "educating students," and "student attitudes"

For project 12.2 "civic engagement and colleges," "student activism," "students and social responsibility," "colleges and social responsibility," and "student movements"

For project 12.3 poverty, hunger, homelessness, unemployment, "town and gown," and "campus and community"

If you are having problems with your searches or the search terms are not producing the desired results, please ask a reference librarian at your school for assistance. Reference librarians are amazing resources and can be a huge help to you as you proceed.

Choose four or five recently published articles that are available in your library that appear relevant to your research question.

Of course none of the articles will answer the research question completely. Each may contribute a little bit of related data or ways of thinking about the question. For each article, note the following:

- Which of your major concepts (e.g., student attitudes, social responsibility, campus and community relations) are discussed?
- What do they find that adds to your knowledge about the question?

Write a two-page summary of the articles you have read. Then, write a one-page paper summarizing what you have learned from the articles that influences your thinking on the question. Have your expectations changed at all? Why or why not? If yes, revise your hypothesis.

❖ STEP 2: OBTAIN YOUR DATA

You have developed a research question and conducted some background work. No doubt your thoughts about what you will find from your research have changed since you first thought about the research question. Now, it's time to obtain the data to test whether your present expectations are on target.

In each of the three guided exercises below, we present a research design appropriate for one of the research projects. Be sure to continue with the project you selected when you began Step 1. You can work individually or in small groups, depending upon what your professor prefers.

Exercise 12.1 **Civic Engagement and Higher Education**

Data Collection Exercise

In this exercise, you will survey at least 30 students to determine (a) how interested students at your school are in learning how to become active, effective members of society; and (b) the extent to which students on your campus are socially active.

1. Go to this book's Web site. Select "Research Tools" and download "survey for research project 12.1"; also download the "scoring guide" for research project 12.1.

2. Determine where and when to find respondents. Do not just haphazardly hand out forms to people. Rather, select a large general education class that will provide a relatively representative sample of the student body (representing students from different years, majors, races, ethnicities, sexes, etc.) Be sure to receive prior permission from the professor teaching the course to hand out your survey at the beginning of one of the class meetings.

3. Ask the students to take a 5–10 minute survey. Read them the instructions and then hand out the survey. Instruct the students not to sign their names and tell them to put the completed surveys face down in a pile. (That way they know you will not be able to connect them with their individual responses.)

4. Follow the instructions in the scoring guide in order to analyze the results. You may want to try grouping your data with those of other students who are also carrying out this project (this will enable you to have a larger sample on which to base your findings). Write a 3–4 page paper that presents and analyzes your results and relates them to the previous research you found on the topic.

Exercise 12.2 **Social Responsibility on Campus**

Data Collection Exercise

In this exercise, you will interview at least 10 students about how socially responsible they believe your school is. You will ask them questions that address both specific indicators of social responsibility and their overall impression of the social responsibility of the school.

1. Go to this book's Web site. Select "Research Tools" and download the interview guidelines, coding guide, and the informed consent statement for research project 12.2.

(Continued)

(Continued)

2. Determine where and when to find respondents. Be sure to interview students who are most likely to know (and care) about your topic (e.g., leaders in student government, club officers, members of student activist groups, student representatives to the Board of Trustees, etc.).

3. Ask the students you select for permission to interview them. Give them the informed consent sheet to read and sign. Ask permission to tape-record the interview. (If they won't allow you to record, you will need to take detailed notes.)

4. Ask them questions about the topics in the interview guidelines. Start with the most general questions, as noted there. But let the subject guide the conversation. Do not try to force all of them to answer the same questions in the same way. However, do make sure they each cover all of the topics in the interview guidelines. The point is to get their individual perspectives and then compare them with one another. A good interviewer asks "probe questions" throughout the interview. These are very short and simple questions such as "Can you expand on that?" "Interesting, what else might you add?" Probe questions give a cue to the person being interviewed to talk more on the subject, while not pushing the interviewee toward your own biases.

5. Follow the instructions in the coding guide to analyze the results. If possible, group your data with those of other students carrying out the same project (this will enable you to have a larger sample on which to base your findings).

6. Write a 3–4 page paper that presents and analyzes your results and relates them to the previous research you found on the topic.

| Exercise 12.3 | Connecting the Campus to the Community |

Data Collection Exercise

Please note: For this project, you can collect data through *either* (a) interviews *or* (b) surveys.

Interviews

You will interview leaders in the local community about the relationship between your school and the community.

1. Go to this book's Web site. Select "Research Tools" and download the interview guidelines, coding guide, and the informed consent statement for Project 12.3.

2. Identify at least three leaders in the local community who would have reason to know the extent and nature of the connection between your school and the college (e.g., the mayor, deputies to the mayor, the city manager, city council members, directors of local non-profit agencies). You can find local non-profit organizations in your area by using World Hunger Year's National Hunger Clearinghouse database (http://www .worldhungeryear.org/nhc_ data/nhc_01.asp), which includes organizations that deal with various issues related to poverty, in addition to hunger). Simply fill in the information, and the database will give you a list of organizations in your area. You can also find such organizations by using the Idealist.org database (http://idealist.org/).

3. Ask each community leader for permission to do the interview. Give him or her the informed consent sheet to read and sign. Ask permission to tape record the interview. (If he or she won't allow you to record it, you will need to take detailed notes.)

4. Ask the community leaders questions about the topics in the interview guidelines. Start with the most general questions, as noted in the guidelines. But let the subject guide the conversation. Do not try to force all the subjects to answer the same questions in the same way. However, do make sure each one covers all of the topics in the interview guidelines. The point is to get their individual perspectives and then compare each perspective with the others. A good interviewer asks "probe questions" throughout the interview. These are very short and simple questions, such as "Can you expand on that?" "Interesting; what else might you add?" Probe questions give a cue to the person being interviewed to talk more on the subject, but they do not push the interviewee toward your own biases.

5. Follow the instructions in the coding guide to analyze the results. If possible, group your data with those of other students carrying out interviews for this project (this will enable you to have a larger sample on which to base your findings).

6. Compare your findings with those of your classmates who collected survey data for this project.

7. Write a 3–4 page paper that presents and analyzes your results (and, if possible, the results of your classmates' interviews), relates them to the previous research you found on the topic, and compares them to the findings of your classmates who conducted surveys on this topic.

(Continued)

(Continued)

Surveys

You will survey at least 30 students in order to measure the (1) attitudes of students toward the local community and (2) the degree of interaction between students and the community.

1. Go to this book's Web site. Select "Research Tools" and download "survey for research project 12.3"; also download the "scoring guide" for Research Project 12.3.

2. Determine where and when to find respondents. Do not just hand out forms to people haphazardly. Select a large general education class that will provide a relatively representative sample of the student body. Be sure to receive prior permission from the professor teaching the course to hand out your survey at the beginning of one of the class meetings.

3. Ask the students to take a 5- to 10-minute survey. Read them the instructions and then hand out the survey. Instruct the students not to sign their names and tell them to put the completed surveys face down in a pile. (That way they know you won't be able to connect them with their individual responses.)

4. Follow the instructions in the scoring guide to analyze the results. If possible, group your data with those of other students carrying out the survey for this project (this will enable you to have a larger sample on which to base your findings).

5. Compare your findings with those of your classmates who conducted interviews for Research Project 12.3.

6. Write a 3–4 page paper that presents and analyzes your results (and, if possible, the results of your classmates' interviews), relates them to the previous research you found on the topic, and compares them to the findings of your classmates who conducted interviews on this topic.

❖   STEP 3: DO SOMETHING ABOUT IT

Now that you have personally investigated an important social issue, you are in a strong position to address it. The following exercises will help you to use your sociological knowledge to make a difference in the lives of people in your community.

Project 12.1	Civic Engagement and Higher Education: Civic Engagement Exercise

From your research, you have some data that indicates how many students think civic engagement should be a part of a college education and how many students are socially active. For this exercise, you will prepare a *talking points* document designed to change the minds of those students who do not think civic engagement should be a part of a college education. You will then organize a campus panel with other students at which you will present your talking points.

A talking points document is a brief summary of relevant issues to help you put things into perspective, to establish a context for your concerns, and to focus on what is most important in your argument. It is also a fact sheet that provides evidence to support your position.

1. Drawing on your knowledge of the topic (through your background reading), list the five most important reasons why students should want civic engagement to be a part of a college education.

2. Using information from your survey data, this book, or published research on the topic, identify the specific reasons why students might *not* want civic engagement to be a part of a college education, and then counter their arguments (e.g., if you think that students will say they don't have time to be socially active, mention the fact that many schools have included civic-engaged activities within courses. If students don't understand how they can benefit from becoming socially active, describe to them the connection between social activism and social power.).

3. Write a one-page summary of the talking points designed to help you communicate your five points to a group of students.

4. Try it out. Bring your talking points to a few friends or relatives and ask them if they will let you briefly discuss why you think civic engagement should be part of the college experience. Think about their responses, criticisms, and suggestions and then change your document in ways that will strengthen it.

5. Prepare a 5-minute presentation based on what you have learned. Consider the reasons why rational and thoughtful people might not want civic engagement as part of a college education and think carefully about what you might say that will address and possibly overcome their hesitations. You can find a great guide to help you in putting together and delivering your speech at http://www.youtham bassadors.com/resources/speaking.html.

(Continued)

(Continued)

6. Work with other students who carried out this project to organize and participate in a student panel presentation for the campus community about the connection between civic engagement and higher education.

Project 12.2	Social Responsibility on Campus: Civic Engagement Exercise

Based on your preparation work, you should have a fairly good idea about what social issues students believe your college or university should be addressing on campus (e.g., sweatshops, right to a living wage, health care benefits, sex discrimination, racism).

1. Write a two-page summary of the issue that most concerns you. Include in it a simple description of (a) what the social issue is, (b) who (which group or groups) is suffering as a result of it, (c) who has the power or authority to change it, and (d) what makes you feel that there is a need to address the social issue in the first place.

2. Rewrite your statement in the form of a two-paragraph letter to the editor of your school paper. Begin the letter with the phrase "we the undersigned. . . ." Work and rework this document until you feel confident that you have included your major points and that you have presented them in a clear and powerful manner.

3. Ask people around campus if they would be willing to join you in signing the letter. Provide a signature list form where they can sign their names, print their names, and optionally identify themselves (student, professor, staff, etc.). Also ask them if they wish to become more active in resolving the injustice. If they do, take their contact information (including their phone numbers and e-mail addresses).

4. If you find that most people do not agree with your letter, stop. Rethink. Have you represented the issue fairly? What are their objections? Are they right? If so, you might want to consider a different issue or a different approach, and start again. If you feel they are wrong, you should consider what you could do differently that might convince them to join your cause.

5. After you have collected at least 20 signatures, send the letter to your school newspaper, to the president of your college, and to any other key people on campus that you have identified as having the power to affect this issue.

6. Call a meeting of the people who want to act on the issue. Discuss what to do and do it. That is, devise an action plan and strategy to take action on your issue. On the following Web sites you can find some excellent resources compiled by other student groups that will help you to write letters, organize meetings, and gain all of the tools you need to work for your issue:

- http://studentsagainstsweatshops.org/docs/organizing.doc
- http://www.thetaskforce.org/downloads/campus/campusman.pdf
- http://www.campusactivism.org/uploads/Papers_no2_v4.qxd.pdf
- http://www.campusactivism.org/uploads/FireItUp.pdf

You may also want to consult such books as *Take More* Action by Marc and Craig Kielburger[2] or *Organizing for Social Change: Midwest Academy— Manual for Activists* by Kimberley A. Bobo and colleagues for some guidelines on how to organize effectively. Michael Gecan's book *Going Public* is also an excellent overview of how to build power through organized people.

Project 12.3	Connecting the Campus to the Community: Civic Engagement Exercise

Identify a few nonprofit groups in your area that are working on poverty-related issues. There may be an office on campus that can help you find one. If you are an active member of a church, mosque, synagogue, or other civic organization, find out how they are addressing poverty in the community. Call your local mayor's office and ask if there are community groups that the city or town works with on poverty-related issues such as hunger, homelessness, and housing. You should also search World Hunger Year's National Hunger Clearinghouse database at http://www.worldhungeryear.org/nhc_data/nhc_01.asp. As we note above, you can simply fill in the information, and the database will give you a list of organizations in your area. You can also find such organizations through the Idealist.org Web site at http://idealist.org/.

1. Visit the organization you have chosen (or visit several if you are having trouble choosing.) Speak with people there, pick up their literature, and search their Web site if they have one. Identify and summarize what their basic work is, how it is organized, and what they want from volunteers. Given your knowledge of the issue, make note of how well the group's work relates to your area of interest.

(Continued)

(Continued)

2. Get to know the group better. Attend a meeting or volunteer for an event. Speak with other volunteers about their experiences.

3. If you are excited by the work of the organization, organize a group of students to volunteer their time and talents to work with them. Tell the other potential volunteers what you know about the issue and what this group is doing. Try to get a meaningful sense of what kind of commitment other students are willing to make, so that you don't promise too much, and offer your services to the group as volunteers.

Two notes of caution should be added before you recruit too many volunteers. First, make sure that you have spoken to the people coordinating the efforts of the organizations to find out what they need. They may need help with staffing, clerical assistance, building repairs, fundraising, or a variety of other tasks. It is very important that they are part of your process! Second, many organizations prefer to start their volunteers off with clerical tasks, like faxing or filing. The point of this exercise is to get your hands dirty and to do something about an ongoing social problem. However, make sure you have a clear sense of what the group wants from you before you commit to doing it.

Sociologist in Action: You!

(Place brief biography and description of your class project here.)

You've now joined the ranks of "Sociologists in Action." Like the work of the "Sociologists in Action" highlighted in this book, your efforts can inspire others to become knowledgeable, engaged, and effective citizens. Although such sociologists may not look like superheroes, they have all managed to harness the power of sociology to make society better. Congratulations on becoming one of them. Please email us your "Sociologist in Action" piece (engagedsociologist@hotmail.com) and let us know if we can use it on our Web site or in future editions of *The Engaged Sociologist: Connecting the Classroom to the Community.*

❖ CONCLUSION

You now have sociological tools, skills, and knowledge. You do not have to be a professional sociologist to use them. Just keep your eyes open to how society is working (the sociological eye), make connections between personal troubles and public issues (the sociological imagination), and always look for multiple perspectives. Ask questions and find your own answers. Change is always happening all around us. Whether or not we choose to help direct it is up to us. We don't know what social problems or issues you will confront in your life, but we do know that you can make a difference. The anthropologist Margaret Mead once said, "Never doubt that a small group of thoughtful, committed citizens can change the world. Indeed, it's the only thing that ever has." Using your sociological tools, *you* can help change the world.

❖ ENDNOTES

1. The Campus Compact and American Democracy Project efforts are a direct result of this growing realization among academic and government leaders. You can find many sources and links to articles about this topic on the Web sites for these organizations (http://www.compact.org/ and http://www.aascu.org/programs/adp/default.htm).

2. Kielburger, Craig and Marc Kielburger. 2004. *Take More Action*. Toronto, ON, Canada: Thomson/Nelson.

❖ REFERENCES

Bobo, Kimberley A., Steve Max, Kim Bobo, Jackie Kendall, and Midwest Academy. 1999. *Organizing for Social Change: Midwest Academy—Manual for Activists*. Santa Ana, CA: Seven Locks Press.

Gecan, Michael. 2004. *Going Public*. New York: Random House.

Kielburger, Marc and Craig Kielburger. 2004. *Take More Action*. Toronto, ON, Canada: Thomson/Nelson.

Index